THE ITIL® V3 MANA
BRIDGE CERTIFIC
IT SERVICE MANA
A Guide for Exam Candidates

BCS The Chartered Institute for IT

BCS The Chartered Institute for IT promotes wider social and economic progress through the advancement of information technology, science and practice. We bring together industry, academics, practitioners and government to share knowledge, promote new thinking, inform the design of new curricula, shape public policy and inform the public. As the professional membership and accreditation body for IT, we serve over 70,000 members including practitioners, academics and students, in the UK and internationally. A leading IT qualification body, we offer a range of widely recognised professional and end-user qualifications.

Joining BCS The Chartered Institute for IT

BCS qualifications, products and services are designed with your career plans in mind. We not only provide essential recognition through professional qualifications but also offer many other useful benefits to our members at every level.

BCS Membership demonstrates your commitment to professional development.

It helps to set you apart from other IT practitioners and provides industry recognition of your skills and experience. Employers and customers increasingly require proof of professional qualifications and competence. Professional membership confirms your competence and integrity and sets an independent standard that people can trust. Professional Membership (MBCS) is the pathway to Chartered IT Professional (CITP) Status.
www.bcs.org/membership

Further Information

BCS The Chartered Institute for IT, First Floor, Block D, North Star House, North Star Avenue, Swindon, SN2 1FA, United Kingdom.
T +44 (0) 1793 417 424
F +44 (0) 1793 417 444
www.bcs.org/contact

THE ITIL® V3 MANAGER'S BRIDGE CERTIFICATE IN IT SERVICE MANAGEMENT
A Guide for Exam Candidates

Colin Rudd

Published by British Informatics Society Limited (BISL), a wholly owned subsidiary of BCS The Chartered Institute for IT, First Floor, Block D, North Star House, North Star Avenue, Swindon, SN2 1FA, UK.
www.bcs.org

ISBN 978-1-906124-20-5

British Cataloguing in Publication Data.
A CIP catalogue record for this book is available at the British Library.

Typeset by Lapiz Digital Services, Chennai, India.
Printed at CPI Antony Rowe Ltd, Chippenham, UK.

CONTENTS

FIGURES AND TABLES

Figures 3.1–3.3, 4.1–4.11, 5.1–5.20, 6.1, 6.3–6.11, 7.1–7.6, 8.1–8.11, 9.1–9.3 & 11.1 are based on OGC ITIL material. Reproduced under licence from OGC.

Tables 6.1 and 6.2 are based on OGC ITIL material. Reproduced under licence from OGC.

AUTHOR

Colin Rudd is an internationally recognised expert in Service Management (SM) and has been working in the Information Technology (IT) industry for over 35 years. During this time Colin has delivered presentations, workshops, consultancy and training in many regions and countries, including the UK, USA, Australia, China, Japan, Singapore, the Middle East and all over Europe. His passion is the implementation and improvement of IT management systems and processes. Colin has helped numerous organisations to implement effective and efficient 'world class' IT management systems that have won quality awards and achieved external certification against international standards.

Colin started his IT life as an analyst/programmer and rapidly progressed to become a technical specialist in operating systems and networking, installing many national, European and international networks, including the Moscow Olympics systems. He subsequently moved into IT and network management and wrote his first book on Network Services Management in 1994 based on his knowledge and experience of the industry. Since then he has been helping organisations to improve all areas of IT management. He has also been instrumental in the development of standard industry qualification and accreditation programmes. These developments have been achieved in conjunction with many of the leading industry bodies and associations, such as BCS, itSMF, OGC, CMA, APMG, EXIN, NCC, BSI, UKAS and the SFIA Foundation. In May 1999, he set up his own IT management consultancy and training services company to further develop his interest and experience in all aspects of network, systems, enterprise and Service Management.

Colin has also worked closely with the British Standards Institute (BSI) and the International Organization for Standardization (ISO) on the development of ISO/IEC 20000, the international standard for IT Service Management. He was the key player behind the development and establishment of the itSMF ISO/IEC 20000 certification and qualification scheme, the leading international scheme within the area of IT Service Management.

Colin has an honours degree in Mathematics and is a chartered engineer, a chartered IT professional and a fellow of BCS, of the Institute of IT Service Management (ISM) and of the Institute of IT Trainers (IIT). He has contributed to the development of both the Industry Structure Model and its successor, the Skills Framework for the Information Age (SFIA). He has also authored and contributed to many books on IT Management and Service Management including authoring of modules in ITIL® versions 1, 2 and 3. He has also written numerous white papers and articles on associated topics.

Recognition as a leading authority on Service Management came in 2002 when Colin was presented with the itSMF's Lifetime Achievement award for contributions to the Service Management industry. Colin has also received awards for business excellence from some of his clients, for the quality of the training and consultancy he has delivered.

"ITIL is a Registered Trademark of the Office of Government Commerce in the United Kingdom and other countries."

ABBREVIATIONS

AMIS	Availability Management Information System
APMG	APM Group
ASP	Application Service Provider
BCS	British Computer Society
BIA	Business Impact Analysis
BPO	Business Process Outsourcing
BRM	Business Relationship Management/Manager
BSI	The British Standards Institute
CAB	Change Advisory Board
CAB/EC	Change Advisory Board/Emergency Committee
CI	Configuration Item
CIO	Chief Information Officer
CMA	The Communications Managers Association
CMDB	Configuration Management Database
CMIS	Capacity Management Information System
CMM	Capability Maturity Model
CMMI®	Capability Maturity Model Integration
CMS	Configuration Management System
COBIT®	Control Objectives for Information and related Technology
CSF	Critical Success Factor
CSI	Continual Service Improvement
CSP	Core Service Package
CTO	Chief Technical Officer
DHS	Definitive Hardware Store
DIKW	Data → Information → Knowledge → Wisdom

DML	Definitive Media Library
DSL	Definitive Software Library
EXIN	The Examinations Institute
FAQ	Frequently Asked Questions
GTB	Grow The Business
IMAC	Installations Moves Additions Changes
ISACA	Information Systems Audit and Control Association
ISEB	Information Systems Examination Board
ISM	Information Security Management
ISMS	Information Security Management System
ISO	International Organization for Standardization
IT	Information Technology
ITSCM	IT Service Continuity Management
ITSM	IT Service Management
itSMF	IT Service Management Forum
ITT	Invitation to Tender
KPI	Key Performance Indicator
KPO	Knowledge Process Outsourcing
LoS	Line of Service
NCC	The National Computer Centre
OGC	The Office of Government Commerce
OLA	Operational Level Agreement
OSI	Open Systems Interconnection
PBA	Pattern of Business Activity
PDCA	Plan → Do → Check → Act
PFS	Prerequisites for Success
RACI	An example of an authority matrix: Responsible, Accountable, Consulted, Informed
RAD	Rapid Application Development
RFC	Request For Change
ROI	Return On Investment
RTB	Run The Business

SaaS	Software as a Service
SAC	Service Acceptance Criterion
SACM	Service Asset and Configuration Management
SCD	Supplier and Contract Database
SCM	Service Catalogue Management
SD	Service Design
SDP	Service Design Package
SEI	Software Engineering Institute
SFIA	Skills Framework for the Information Age
SIP	Service Improvement Plan
SKMS	Service Knowledge Management System
SLA	Service Level Agreement
SLM	Service Level Management
SLP	Service Level Package
SLR	Service Level Requirement
SM	Service Management
SMART	Specific-Measurable-Achievable-Relevant-Timely
SMIS	Security Management Information System
SO	Service Operation
SOA	Service-Oriented Architecture
SOR	Statement of Requirement
SPM	Service Portfolio Management
SS	Service Strategy
SSU	Shared Services Unit
ST	Service Transition
TCO	Total Cost of Ownership
TQM	Total Quality Management
TTB	Transform The Business
UKAS	UK Accreditation Service
UP	User Profile
VOI	Value On Investment
WIP	Work in Progress

GLOSSARY†

Alert A warning that a threshold has been reached, something has changed or
a failure has occurred.

Architecture The fundamental organisation of a system, embodied in its
components, their relationships to each other and to the environment and the
principles guiding its design and evolution.

Business Case Justification for a significant item of expenditure. Includes
information about costs, benefits, options, issues, risks and possible problems.

Business Unit A segment of the business which has its own plans, metrics,
income and costs. Each Business Unit owns assets and uses these to create value
for customers in the form of goods and services.

Capabilities The ability of an organisation, person, process, application,
configuration item or IT service to carry out an activity. Capabilities are
intangible assets of an organisation.

Configuration Item A Configuration Item (CI) is any component that needs to
be managed in order to deliver an IT service. Information about each CI is
recorded in a configuration record within the Configuration Management System
and is maintained throughout its lifecycle by Configuration Management. CIs
are under the control of Change Management. CIs typically include IT services,
hardware, software, buildings, people and formal documentation such as process
documentation and SLAs. CIs should be selected using established selection
criteria, grouped, classified and identified in such a way that they are
manageable and traceable throughout the Service Lifecycle.

Configuration Management Database A Configuration Management
Database (CMDB) stores configuration records containing Attributes of CIs and
their relationships. A CMS may include one or more CMDBs.

Configuration Management System A Configuration Management System
(CMS) is a set of tools and databases that are used to manage an IT service
provider's configuration data. The CMS also includes information about
Incidents, Problems, known errors, changes and releases, and may contain data
about employees, suppliers, locations, Business Units, customers and users. The
CMS includes tools for collecting, storing, managing, updating and presenting

data about all Configuration Items and their relationships. The CMS is maintained by Configuration Management and is used by all IT Service Management Processes.

Configuration Model A Configuration Model is a model of the services, assets and the infrastructure that includes relationships between CIs, enabling other processes to access valuable information (e.g. assessing the impact of Incidents, Problems and proposed changes; planning and designing new or changed services and their release and deployment; optimising asset utilisation and costs).

Core Service An IT service that delivers basic outcomes desired by one or more customers.

Customer Portfolio A database or structured document used to record all customers of the IT service provider. The Customer Portfolio is Business Relationship Management's view of the customers who receive services from the IT service provider.

Definitive Media Library A Definitive Media Library (DML) is one or more locations in which the definitive and approved versions of all software CIs are securely stored. The DML may also contain associated CIs such as licences and documentation. The DML is a single logical storage area even if there are multiple locations. All software in the DML is under the control of Change and Release Management and is recorded in the Configuration Management System. Only software from the DML is acceptable for use in a release.

Deployment Deployment is the activity responsible for the movement of new or changed hardware, software, documentation, process etc. to the Live Environment.

Emergency change A change that must be introduced as soon as possible. For example to resolve a Major Incident or implement a security patch. The Change Management process will normally have a specific procedure for handling emergency changes.

Enterprise Architecture The process of translating business vision and strategy into effective enterprise change, by creating, communicating and improving key principles and models that describe the enterprise's future states and enable its evolution. (Gartner definition)

Event A change of state that has significance for the management of a Configuration Item or IT service.

Function A team or group of people and the tools they use to carry out one or more Processes or activities (e.g. the Service Desk or IT Operations).

Incident An Incident is an unplanned interruption to an IT service or reduction in the quality of an IT service. Failure of a Configuration Item that has not yet impacted service is also an Incident.

Key Performance Indicator   Only the most important metrics are defined as KPIs. KPIs should be selected to ensure that Efficiency, Effectiveness and Cost-Effectiveness are all managed.

Line of Service (LoS)   A Core Service or Supporting Service that has multiple Service Level Packages. A LoS is managed by a Product Manager and each Service Level Package is designed to support a particular market segment.

Market Space   All opportunities that an IT service provider could exploit to meet the business needs of customers. The Market Space identifies the possible IT services that an IT service provider may wish to consider delivering.

Metric   Something that is measured and reported to help manage a Process, IT Service or Activity.

Normal change   A change that follows normal change procedures.

Operational Level Agreement   An Operational Level Agreement (OLA) is an agreement between an IT service provider and another part of the same organisation. An OLA supports the IT service provider's delivery of IT services to the customers. The OLA defines the goods or services to be provided and the responsibilities of both parties.

Pattern of Business Activity (PBA)   A workload profile of one or more business activities. PBAs are used to help the service provider understand and plan for different levels of business activity.

Problem   A Problem is the cause of one or more Incidents.

Process   A Process is a structured set of activities designed to accomplish a specific objective.

Process Manager   A role responsible for operational management of a Process. The Process Manager's responsibilities include planning and coordination of all activities required to carry out, monitor and report on the Process.

Process Owner   A role responsible for ensuring that a process is fit for purpose. The Process Owner's responsibilities include sponsorship, design, change management and continual improvement of the Process and its metrics.

Release   A Release is a collection of hardware, software, documents, processes or other components required to implement one or more approved Changes to IT services. The contents of each Release are managed, tested and deployed as a single entity.

Release Unit   Components of an IT service that are normally released together. A Release Unit typically includes sufficient components to perform a useful function.

Resource A generic term that includes IT infrastructure, people, money or anything else that might help to deliver an IT service. Resources are considered to be assets of an organisation.

Risk A risk is a possible event that could cause harm or loss, or affect the ability to achieve objectives. A risk is measured by the probability of a threat, the vulnerability of the asset to that threat, and the impact it would have if it occurred.

Role A set of responsibilities, activities and authorities granted to a person or team. A Role is defined in a Process. One person or team may have multiple roles (e.g. the roles of Configuration Manager and Change Manager may be carried out by a single person).

Service A service is a means of delivering value to customers by facilitating outcomes that customers want to achieve without the ownership of specific costs and risks.

Service Assets Any capability or resource of a service provider.

Service Catalogue A database or structured document with information about all live IT services, including those available for deployment. The Service Catalogue is the only part of the Service Portfolio published to customers and is used to support the sale and delivery of IT services.

Service Change The addition, modification or removal of authorised, planned or a supported Service or service component and its associated documentation.

Service Design Package Document(s) defining all aspects of an IT service and its requirements through each stage of its Lifecycle. A Service Design Package is produced for each new IT service, major change, or IT service retirement.

Service Knowledge Management System (SKMS) A set of tools and databases that are used to manage knowledge and information. The SKMS includes the Configuration Management System, as well as other tools and databases. The SKMS stores, manages, updates and presents all information that an IT service provider needs to manage the full lifecycle of IT services.

Service Level Agreement ITIL defines a Service Level Agreement (SLA) as an agreement between an IT service provider and a customer. The SLA describes the IT service, records service level targets and specifies the responsibilities for the IT service provider and the customer. A single SLA may cover multiple IT services or multiple customers.

Service Level Package (SLP) A defined level of Utility and Warranty for a particular Service Package. Each SLP is designed to meet the needs of a particular Pattern of Business Activity.

Service Management   Service Management is a set of specialised organisational capabilities for providing value to customers in the form of services.

Service Owner   A role which is accountable for the delivery of a specific IT Service.

Service Package   A detailed description of an IT service that is available to be delivered to customers. A Service Package includes a Service Level Package (SLP) and one or more Core Services and Supporting Services.

Service Pipeline   A database or structured document listing all IT services that are under consideration or development, but are not yet available to customers. The Service Pipeline provides a business view of possible future IT services and is part of the Service Portfolio which is not normally published to customers.

Service Portfolio   The complete set of services that are managed by a service provider. The Service Portfolio is used to manage the entire lifecycle of all services, and includes three categories: Service Pipeline (proposed or in Development); Service Catalogue (live or available for deployment); and Retired Services.

Service Portfolio Management (SPM)   The process responsible for managing the Service Portfolio. Service Portfolio Management considers services in terms of the business value that they provide.

Service Provider   An organisation supplying services to one or more internal customers or external customers.

Service Request   A request from a user for information, or advice, or for a standard change or for access to an IT service. For example to reset a password or to provide standard IT services for a new user. Service Requests are usually handled by a Service Desk and do not require a Request for Change (RFC) to be submitted.

Standard change   A Standard change is a pre-approved change that is low risk, relatively common and follows a Procedure or Work Instruction. For example password reset or provision of standard equipment to a new employee. RFCs are not required to implement a standard change, and they are logged and tracked using a different mechanism, such as a Service Request.

Strategic asset   Strategic assets are assets that provide the basis for core competence, distinctive performance, durable advantage and qualifications to participate in business opportunities. IT organisations can use the guidance provided by ITIL to transform their Service Management capabilities into strategic assets.

Supporting Service   A service that enables or enhances a Core Service. For example a Directory Service or a Backup Service.

System A collection of components organised to accomplish a specific function or set of functions.

Utility Functionality offered by a product or service to meet a particular need.

Value Network A value network is a web of relationships that generates tangible and intangible value through complex dynamic exchanges through two or more organisations.

Warning A warning is an event that is generated when a service or device is approaching a threshold.

Warranty A promise or guarantee that a product or service will meet its agreed requirements.

INTRODUCTION

NATURE AND PURPOSE OF THE BOOK

This book provides candidates with information to help them with their study and preparation for the ITIL Manager's Bridge Examination.

PURPOSE OF THE MANAGER'S BRIDGE EXAM CERTIFICATE

The Manager's Bridge qualification will bridge the gap between the ITIL Manager's Certificate in IT Service Management and the ITIL Expert in IT Service Management. This course is intended only for those holding a valid ITIL Manager's Certificate in IT Service Management ITIL versions 1 and 2. Students wishing to progress to the ITIL Master in IT Service Management must provide documentary evidence of attaining this qualification (and the earlier Manager's Certificate) before being allow to progress to the Master level.

Target group
Those targeted by the ITIL Manager's Bridge Qualification are individuals who already hold the Manager's Certificate in IT Service Management at an earlier ITIL version and who wish to obtain the ITIL Expert in IT Service Management, thereby demonstrating their knowledge of ITIL v3.

This may include, but is not limited to, Chief Information Officers (CIOs), Senior IT Managers, IT Managers and Supervisors, IT professionals and IT Operation practitioners.

Learning objectives
Candidates can expect to gain the following competencies:

- An understanding of the background of ITIL v3 and why ITIL needed to change.

- An understanding of the value of IT Service Management (ITSM) Good Practice and an ability to define and describe a Service and the concept of Service Management as a practice.

- An understanding of the Service Lifecycle and of the objectives and business value for each stage in the Lifecycle.

- The ability to comprehend and articulate some of the key terminology and explain the key concepts of Service Management. Candidates should also be able to show how these concepts can be used as part of a successful ITSM project or in successful operation of ITSM processes.

- An ability to comprehend and communicate the key principles and models of Service Management and to balance some of the opposing forces within Service Management.

- An understanding of how the Service Management processes contribute to the Service Lifecycle; explaining the objectives, scope, concepts, activities, key metrics (Key Performance Indicators), roles and challenges for all of the ITIL v3 processes; explaining the role, objectives, organisational structures, staffing and metrics of the ITIL v3 functions.

- An understanding of each role and the responsibilities of each of the roles in Service Management.

- An understanding of the planning and implementation of Service Management technologies, the requirements for an integrated set of Service Management technology and how automation assists the integration of Service Management processes.

- A sufficient understanding of the implementation considerations to enable them to contribute to such implementations.

- An understanding of how ITIL v3 interfaces and can be used alongside complementary industry guidance.

Entry criteria

This qualification is available **only** to candidates who already hold the Manager's Certificate in IT Service Management. The examination has been written on the basis that in preparing for the examination all candidates will have attended an accredited training course and will have read the ITIL Service Lifecycle Practices core guidance which includes:

- Service Strategy (SS);
- Service Design (SD);
- Service Transition (ST);
- Service Operation (SO);
- Continual Service Improvement (CSI);
- Introduction to the Service Lifecycle (optional, but recommended).

THE MANAGER'S BRIDGE SYLLABUS

The syllabus will guide the design, development and use of training materials as well as training aimed at raising understanding of, and competence in, IT Service Management as described in the ITIL Service Strategy, ITIL Service Design, ITIL Service Transition, ITIL Service Operation, ITIL Continual Service Improvement,

ITIL Introduction and ITIL Glossary publications. The syllabus has been designed for ease of reference, extensibility and ease of maintenance in mind.

The Manager's Bridge syllabus is based on the Foundation bridging syllabus (as the Manager's Bridge training and qualification encompasses the Foundation Bridge. Candidates already qualified at Manager's level do not therefore have to separately attend the Foundation Bridge.) The syllabus, however, is broader and will train and test skills at a greater depth of understanding, appropriate to a Manager's level qualification.

The main focus of the Manager's Bridge will be the new content of ITIL v3 and those things that have changed. The syllabus is therefore in two parts:

- Part 1 covers those things that are new to ITIL v3 and that will form the main focus for the qualification.
- Part 2 covers those things that were well known at v2, but with some significant differences. The training/qualification will focus only on those elements that have changed.

Candidates for the ITIL Manager's Bridge qualification must complete the 10 units of study detailed within the Manager's Bridge course syllabus and successfully pass the relevant complex multiple choice examination to achieve certification. The units cover these topics:

- Introduction;
- The Service Lifecycle;
- General concepts and definitions;
- Key principles and models;
- Processes;
- Functions;
- Roles and organisation;
- Technology and architecture;
- Implementation considerations;
- Complementary industry guidance.

The latest version of the syllabus can be found at http://www.bcs.org//upload/pdf/itilv3-mc-bridge-itsm-syllabus.pdf.

Note: The minimum study (contact) time totals 28 hrs. It is envisaged that providers will offer this as a four-day course and use innovative ways of presenting the material, including exercises and assignments to re-enforce the knowledge gained. A mock examination will be made available to assist in examination preparation. Training providers are free to structure and organise their training in a way they find most appropriate, providing the units below are covered.

Format of the examination

Type: Twenty (20) question Scenario-based, complex multiple-choice examination.

Duration: 90 minutes. Candidates sitting the examination in a language other than their native language have a maximum of 120 minutes and are allowed the use of a dictionary.

Prerequisite: Manager's Certificate in IT Service Management

Supervised: Yes

Open-book: No

Pass Score: 80% (16 of 20)

Distinction Score: No

Delivery: Online or paper-based via an Accredited Training Organisation.

RELATIONSHIP OF THE BOOK TO THE SYLLABUS

This book is closely aligned to the structure of the syllabus, but differs in some areas. This is to help the reader study the material. Logical subject matter is grouped together in one study unit rather than separating it as is done within the syllabus. However, syllabus references are clearly contained within the text at the appropriate points to help cross reference with the syllabus document itself.

HOW TO GET THE BEST OUT OF THIS BOOK

This book is designed to be used by different groups of people. It can be used either as a learning aid for self study or as reference/revision aid to support course material within an accredited training course.

Before using the book as a learning aid, candidates need to familiarise themselves with the syllabus structure and content.

Those candidates using the book as a reference or revision aid while completing an accredited course will be guided through the use of the book by the course tutor. If you are using the book for final revision before sitting the exam, you should first try and identify those areas where you feel weakest.

1   OVERVIEW

LEARNING OBJECTIVES

The purpose of this chapter is to help candidates understand the background for ITIL v3 and why ITIL needed to change. Specifically, candidates must be able to:

- understand and explain the background to the new ITIL version and how the project got input from different stakeholder groups and nationalities;
- understand and explain why ITIL needed to change;
- understand and explain the new structure of ITIL (core, complementary and web-based material).

UNDERSTANDING ITIL V3

ITIL was originally called the IT Infrastructure Library, but has now come to be known simply as ITIL. Initially produced in the 1980s and early 1990s as a set of over 40 books covering various IT processes and practices, it was restructured between 1999 and 2006 as a revised set of seven core books:

- Service Support;
- Service Delivery;
- Planning to Implement Service Management;
- ICT Infrastructure Management;
- Business Perspective;
- Application Management;
- Security Management.

In order to ensure that ITIL continues to remain relevant and meet the needs of the industry and users it has been extended as shown in Figure 1.1 and explained in the following bullet list.

- The five core books and an official introductory book:
  - Service Strategy;
  - Service Design;

- Service Transition;
- Service Operation;
- Continual Service Improvement.

 Figure 1.1 ITIL complementary products

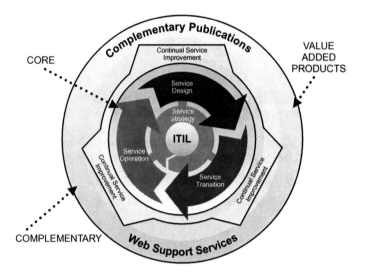

 • Complementary publications: adding value to the core volumes, covering guidance on specific <u>industry sectors,</u> organisation types and technologies and architectures, including:

  - pocket reference books;
  - case studies;
  - ITIL working templates;
  - governance methods;
  - study aids aligned with ITIL qualifications and certifications.

• ITIL Web Support Services: providing online information including value added products, process maps and document templates.

SYLLABUS REFERENCE: ITILMD00-3

Understand and explain the new structure of ITIL (core, complementary and web-based material).

UNDERSTANDING WHY ITIL NEEDED TO CHANGE

An ITIL Refresh Programme sponsored by the Office of Government Commerce (OGC) was launched in 2004 to update the library once more. Supported by many industry groups and associations, an extensive International authoring and quality assurance programme was completed resulting in the five core books that constitute the current version of ITIL.

An overall ITIL Refresh Programme Board was established consisting of:

- OGC representatives: the sponsors and providers of the programme funding;
- itSMF representatives: the IT Service Management Forum representing the major subject matter experts from all of the principal stakeholder groups and countries from around the world;
- TSO representatives: The Stationery Office, the official publishers of the books;
- ISO representatives: supporting the alignment of ISO standards with ITIL;
- Examination Board representatives: from BCS/ISEB, EXIN and APMG representing the qualifications interests;
- The Chief Editor;
- The Chief Architect.

SYLLABUS REFERENCE: ITILMD00-1

Understand and explain the background for the new ITIL v3 and how the project got input from different stakeholder groups and nationalities.

The ITIL Refresh Programme was instigated to ensure that it was kept up to date and continued to meet the needs of the industry and the needs of business, customers and users, especially by:

- improving the consistency, structure and comprehensiveness;
- focusing on outcomes, service value and business integration;
- taking an holistic approach to services and all stages of the Service Lifecycle, particularly in the area of strategy;
- improved alignment with other frameworks and standards, such as COBIT®, CMMI®, SOA and ISO/IEC 20000;
- improved alignment and consistency with recent developments within the IT industry.

SYLLABUS REFERENCE: ITILMD00-2

Understand and explain why ITIL needed to change.

2 SERVICE MANAGEMENT AS A PRACTICE

LEARNING OBJECTIVES

The purpose of this chapter is to help candidates understand the background for ITIL v3 and why ITIL needed to change.

Specifically, candidates must be able to:

- describe the concept of Good Practice and explain and justify how this can assist an organisation;
- define and explain the concept of a service;
- define and explain the concept of Service Management.

THE CONCEPT OF GOOD PRACTICE — APPOPRIATE TO ORG etc.

IT organisations operate in dynamic environments with a need to learn and adapt. In order to improve, organisations often benchmark their capabilities against leading organisations, standards, frameworks and industry practice to identify gaps and opportunities. One way to close such gaps is the adoption of good practices in wide industry use.

However, there are many sources of good practice, including public frameworks, standards and the proprietary knowledge that exists within organisations. Service management as contained within ITIL is 'best practice' and has developed over many years based on a collection of good industry practice from many organisations around the world.

Public frameworks and standards are attractive when compared with proprietary knowledge:

- Proprietary knowledge is deeply embedded in organisations and therefore difficult to adopt, replicate or transfer. Such knowledge is often in the form of tacit knowledge, which is often poorly documented. It is often customised for the local context and specific business needs to the point of being idiosyncratic. Unless the recipients of such knowledge have matching circumstances, the knowledge may not be as effective and often the owners of such information expect to be rewarded for making the knowledge available.

- Publicly available frameworks and standards such as ITIL, COBIT®, ISO 9000, ISO/IEC 20000 and ISO/IEC 27001 are validated across a diverse set of environments and situations rather than the limited experience of a single organisation. They are subject to broad review and diverse use by many organisations and disciplines.

- The knowledge of public frameworks is more likely to be widely distributed among a large community of professionals through publicly available training and certification. Ignoring public frameworks and standards can needlessly place an organisation at a disadvantage. Organisations should cultivate their own proprietary knowledge on top of a body of knowledge based on public frameworks and standards. Collaboration and coordination across organisations are easier because of shared practices and standards.

Good practice is the amalgamation of the best activities from many different organisations.

SYLLABUS REFERENCE: ITILMD01-1

Describe the concept of Good Practice and justify how this can assist an organisation.

 ## THE CONCEPT OF SERVICE MANAGEMENT AS A PRACTICE

The primary objective of Service Management is to deliver value to the business in the form of services.

The value of a service is determined by:

- what the customer prefers (preferences);
- what the customer perceives (perceptions);
- what the customer gets (business outcomes).

The act of transforming resources into valuable services is at the core of Service Management.

'People do not want quarter inch drills. They want quarter inch holes.' (Theodore Levitt)

Customers do not want services or technology. They want fulfilment of particular requirements. Therefore the set of services provided should provide business outcomes that align with business needs and support business processes. What customers value is often different from what the IT provider delivers.

KEY MESSAGE

'Mind the gap.'

Customers also want quality services and products from their suppliers and service providers.

'Quality in a product or service is not what the supplier puts in. It is what the customer gets out and is willing to pay for.' (Peter Ducker)

 WHAT IS SERVICE MANAGEMENT?

SERVICE MANAGEMENT (ITIL) ⟨ FUNCTIONS / PROCESSES / ROLES

Service Management is a set of specialised organisational capabilities for providing value to customers in the form of services.

These organisational capabilities are principally the necessary functions and processes developed by the organisation for the management of services throughout their lifecycle. These capabilities take the form of functions and processes for managing services over a lifecycle, with specialisations in strategy, design, transition, operation and continual improvement. The capabilities represent a service organisation's capacity, competency and confidence for action.

Service Management is a professional practice supported by an extensive body of knowledge, experience and skills. A global community of individuals and organisations in the public and private sectors fosters its growth and maturity.

SYLLABUS REFERENCE: ITILMD01-3

Define and explain the concept of Service Management.

SERVICE

A service is a means of delivering value to customers by facilitating outcomes customers want to achieve without the ownership of specific costs and risks.

Outcomes are possible from the performance of tasks and are limited by the presence of certain constraints. Services facilitate outcomes by enhancing the performance and/or by reducing the effect of constraints. The result is an increase in the possibility of desired outcomes. While some services enhance performance of tasks, others actually perform the task itself. Customers seek outcomes but do not wish to have accountability for all the associated costs and risks.

SYLLABUS REFERENCE: ITILMD01-2

Define and explain the concept of a service.

ITIL provides best practice advice and guidance to all organisations and individuals involved in the provision of IT services to businesses and customers. The library contains a body of knowledge within the core volumes that can be used and applied by any service provider organisation to improve the quality of services they deliver. The information is not prescriptive, but can be used, 'adopted and adapted' to suit any organisation large or small, irrespective of nationality or culture.

 ### KEY MESSAGE

'Adapt and adopt.'

SYLLABUS REFERENCE: ITILMD01-1

Describe the concept of Good Practice and justify how this can assist an organisation.

3 THE SERVICE LIFECYCLE

LEARNING OBJECTIVES

The purpose of this chapter is to help candidates to fully understand the Service Lifecycle.

Specifically, candidates must be able to:

- fully understand and explain the Service Lifecycle;
- describe the structure, scope, and components of ITIL;
- understand and explain the main goals of each stage of the Service Lifecycle;
- fully comprehend and communicate what value each stage provides to the business.

THE STAGES WITHIN THE SERVICE LIFECYCLE

ITIL is based on the Service Lifecycle, with each ITIL core book containing details of one of the stages within the Lifecycle (see Figure 3.1).

The Service Lifecycle consists of five stages from Service Strategy, through Service Design, Service Transition and Service Operation, to Continual Service Improvement. Each publication details the capabilities that have a direct impact on the service provider's performance and provides the necessary guidance for an integrated approach within each of the stages of the Service Lifecycle:

- **Service Strategy** provides guidance on how to design, develop and implement Service Management, not only as an organisational capability, but also as a 'strategic asset'. The book includes topics covering the development of markets (internal and external), Service Assets, the Service Catalogue and implementation of strategy through the Service Lifecycle. Financial Management, Service Portfolio Management, Organisational Development and Strategic Risks are among other major topics that are also explained. Organisations can use the guidance to set policies, objectives and expectations of performance towards serving customers and Market Spaces, and to generate strategies and identify, select and prioritise opportunities.

Figure 3.1 The ITIL core books (Source: OGC ITIL Service Strategy ISBN 978-0-113310-45-6)

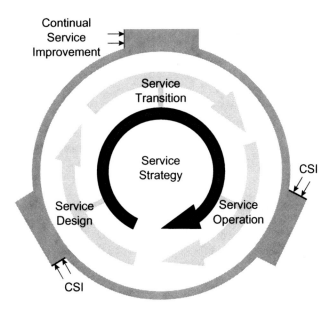

- **Service Design** provides guidance for the design and development of services and Service Management processes. The book includes topics covering design principles and methods for converting strategic objectives into portfolios of services and Service Assets. The scope of Service Design is not limited to new services. It includes the changes and improvements necessary to increase or maintain value to customers during the Service Lifecycle, the continuity of services, achievement of service levels and conformance to standards and regulations. Organisations can use the guidance to develop their design capabilities for Service Management.

- **Service Transition** provides guidance for the development and improvement of capabilities for transitioning new and changed services into operations. The book includes topics covering guidance on how the requirements of Service Strategy and Service Design can be realised in Service Operation while controlling the risks of failure and disruption by applying Change and Release Management, Programme Management and Risk Management techniques. Organisations can use the guidance to manage the complexity of changes to services and Service Management processes, preventing undesired consequences while allowing for innovation.

- **Service Operation** provides guidance on effective and efficient practices in service operation for the delivery and support of services to ensure value for both the customers and the service provider, by achieving strategic objectives making Service Operation a critical capability. The book includes topics covering guidance on how to maintain stability in Service Operation, allowing for changes in design, scale, scope and service levels, and detailed process guidelines, methods and tools for use in two major control perspectives: reactive and proactive. Organisations can use the guidance to improve decision-making in areas such as managing the availability of services, controlling demand, optimising capacity utilisation, scheduling operations and fixing problems.

- **Continual Service Improvement** provides instrumental guidance in creating and maintaining value for customers through better design, transition and operation of services. The book includes topics covering guidance on principles, practices and methods from quality management, Change Management and capability improvement. Organisations can use the guidance to learn to realise incremental and large-scale improvements in service quality, operational efficiency and business continuity and for linking improvement efforts and outcomes with service strategy, design, transition and operation.

Previous to this refresh of ITIL, many organisations only applied Service Management practices and processes to the transition and operation stages of the Service Lifecycle. However, mature organisations made Service Management an integral part of their strategy thus ensuring that the design of service solutions included all of the requirements to deliver the expected business outcomes from the outset.

LIFECYCLE AND SYSTEMS THINKING

Feedback is used to sample the output of processes and systems to influence future action, and structure is essential for organising unrelated information (see Figure 3.2). Without structure our Service Management knowledge is a collection of observations, practices and conflicting goals. The structure of the Lifecycle is an organising framework. Processes describe how things change, whereas structure describes how they are connected. Without structure it is difficult to learn from experience. The Service Lifecycle is an approach to Service Management seeking to understand its structure, the interconnections between the components and how changes will affect the whole system and its constituent components over time.

Figure 3.2 Today's problem is often created by yesterday's solution (Source: OGC ITIL Service Strategy ISBN 978-0-113310-45-6)

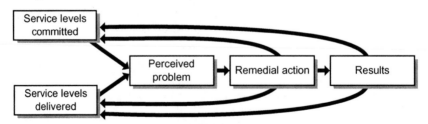

In order to achieve this structure and feedback, all of the processes and activities within the Service Lifecycle need to be linked together in a coherent structure with defined and agreed interfaces, inputs and outputs as shown in Figure 3.3.

Figure 3.3 The key links, inputs and outputs within the Service Lifecycle (Source: OGC ITIL Service Design ISBN 978-0-113310-47-0)

KNOW WHAT'S IN EACH STAGE.

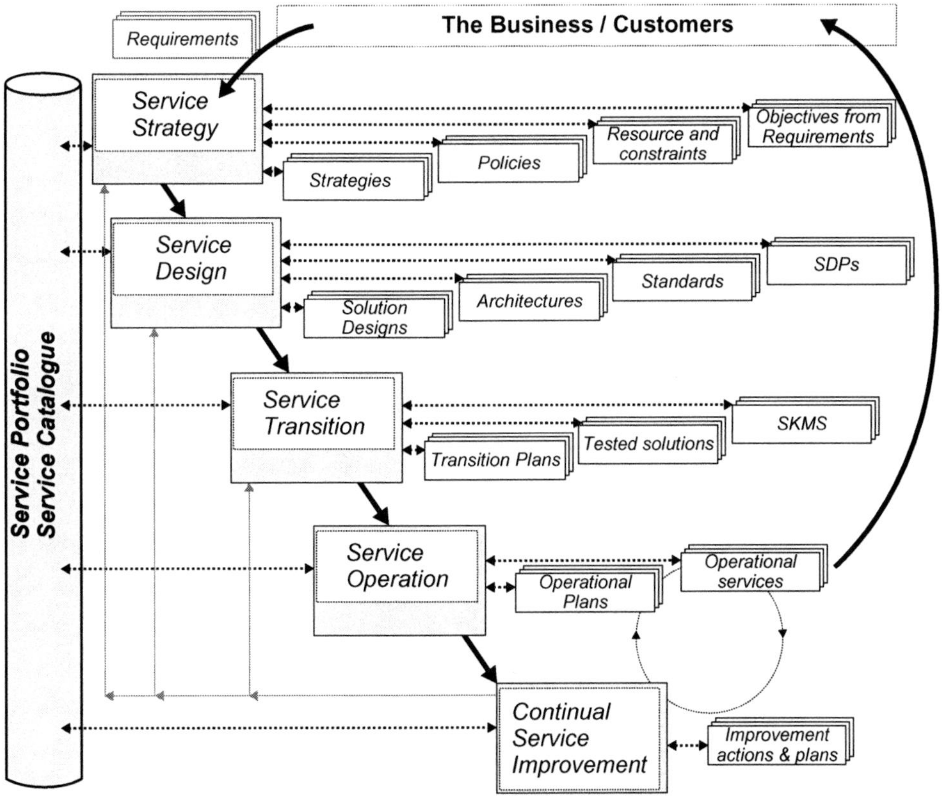

This diagram shows Service Strategy producing the strategies, policies, resource, constraints, requirements and objectives to Service Design. Service Design takes those outputs and designs service solutions, the details of which are contained within Service Design Packages (SDPs) which are passed to Service Transition. From these SDPs, Service Transition develops Transition and Test Plans to validate and test the solutions for deployment to the live environment. Once evaluated and approved, the new services are transitioned to the live environment to be delivered by Service Operation to the business, customers and users. Continual Service Improvement monitors, measures and improves their performance through continual implementation of improvement actions and plans.

SYLLABUS REFERENCE: ITILMD02-1

Fully understand and explain the Service Lifecycle.

SYLLABUS REFERENCE: ITILMD02-2

Describe the structure, scope, components and interfaces of the ITIL Library.

4 GENERIC CONCEPTS AND DEFINITIONS

LEARNING OBJECTIVES

The purpose of this chapter is to help candidates understand the generic concepts and definitions contained within the Service Management modules. Specifically, candidates must be able to define and explain the following key concepts:

- Utility and Warranty;
- Resources and Capabilities;
- the Service Portfolio;
- the role of IT Governance across the Service Lifecycle;
- Business Cases;
- Service Models;
- the Service Design Package;
- the Configuration Management System;
- the Service Knowledge Management System;
- the role of communication in Service Operation;
- the RACI model;
- Risk Management;
- generic roles.

UTILITY AND WARRANTY

From the customer perspective, value consists of two primary elements: Utility and Warranty.

Utility is often summarised as 'what the service does'. It is what the customer gets and can also be referred to as 'the service is fit for purpose'. It is perceived by the customer as the positive effect that a service has on the performance improvement of tasks associated with the desired outcomes. Removal or relaxation of constraints on performance is also perceived as a positive effect.

UTILITY

The functionality offered by a product or service to meet a particular need.

Warranty can be summarised as 'how the service is delivered' and can also be referred to as 'the service is fit for use'. The warranty of a service is defined in terms of the service availability, capacity, security and continuity.

WARRANTY

A promise or guarantee that a product or service will meet its agreed requirements.

The value of a service is always based on, and defined within, the context of the customers and the customer assets. The value of a service is dependent on the combination of both the Utility and Warranty of the service being delivered. Both are necessary. Neither is sufficient by itself, as shown in Figure 4.1.

Figure 4.1 The logic of value creation through services [Source: OGC ITIL Service Strategy ISBN 978-0-113310-45-6]

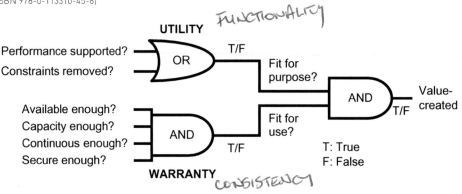

A service provider must ensure that services delivered to the customer are both 'fit for purpose' (Utility) and 'fit for use' (Warranty).

SYLLABUS REFERENCE: ITILMD03-1

Define and explain Utility and Warranty.

RESOURCES AND CAPABILITIES

Resources and Capabilities are Service Assets used by an organisation to create value for customers in the form of services. Resources are used to deliver IT services.

RESOURCES

A generic term that includes IT infrastructure, people, money or anything else that might help to deliver an IT service. Resources are considered to be assets of an organisation.

Capability is the ability to perform an activity or to control and deploy resources to create value.

CAPABILITIES

The ability of an organisation, person, process, application, configuration item or IT service to carry out an activity. Capabilities are intangible assets of an organisation.

Resources are relatively easy to acquire, whereas Capability is often more difficult for an organisation to acquire. Infrastructure and applications can be purchased quite quickly, whereas knowledge and processes take significant time and effort to develop. Service Assets consist of Resources and Capabilities as shown in Table 4.1.

Table 4.1 Resources and Capabilities

Resources	Capabilities
Financial capital	Management
Infrastructure	Organisation
Applications	Process
Information	Knowledge
People (# of)	People (what they can do)

SYLLABUS REFERENCE: ITILMD03-2

Define and explain Resources and Capabilities.

THE SERVICE PORTFOLIO

The Service Portfolio is the most critical management system used to support all of the Service Management processes and describes a service provider's services in terms of business value to the organisation. It articulates business needs and the service provider's response to those needs. Each organisation should carefully design the structure, content and access levels of the Service Portfolio. The content of the Service Portfolio should include:

- service name and description;
- service status classification and criticality;
- applications and data used;
- business processes supported;
- business owners and business users;
- IT owner;
- service warranty level, Service Level Agreements (SLAs) and Service Level Requirements (SLRs);
- supporting services and supporting resources;
- dependent services;
- supporting Operational Level Agreements (OLAs), contracts and agreements;
- service costs, service charges (if applicable) and service revenue (if applicable);
- service metrics.

The Service Portfolio contains the Service Pipeline which contains details of all the services that are under construction or development. The Service Catalogue is also a subset of the Service Portfolio. It is the area of the Service Portfolio which is visible to customers. It consists of live services and those approved to be developed for delivery to current or prospective customers (see Figure 4.2).

Services can enter the Service Catalogue only after due diligence has been performed on related costs and risks. The Catalogue is useful in developing suitable solutions for customers from one or more services. The Service Catalogue is an important tool for Service Strategy because it is the virtual projection of the service provider's actual and present capabilities. It communicates and defines the policies, guidelines and accountability required for Service Portfolio Management (SPM). It defines the criteria for what services fall under SPM and the objective of each service. As service providers may have many customers or serve many businesses, there may be multiple Service Catalogues projected from the Service Portfolio.

Figure 4.2 Service Pipeline and Service Catalogue (Source: OGC ITIL Service Strategy ISBN 978-0-113310-45-6)

Size of bubble reflects level of resources

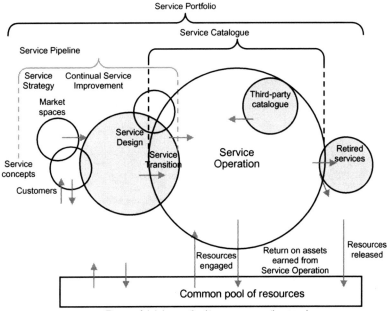

The area of circle is proportional to resources currently engaged In the lifecycle phase (Service Portfolio and Financial Management)

In other words, a Service Catalogue is an expression of the provider's operational capability within the context of a customer or Market Space.

MARKET SPACE — *if to strategy.*

All opportunities that an IT service provider could exploit to meet the business needs of customers. The Market Space identifies the possible IT services that an IT service provider may wish to consider delivering.

The contents of the Service Portfolio and the Service Catalogue and the links between them are shown in Figure 4.3.

Once a strategic decision to approve a service is made, then the service passes to the Service Design stage of the Service Lifecycle. The Service Portfolio should contain information relating to every service and its current status within the organisation. The options of status within the Service Portfolio should include:

- **Requirements:** a set of outline requirements have been received from the business or IT for a new or changed service;
- **Defined:** the set of requirements for the new service are being assessed, defined and documented and the SLR is being produced;

Figure 4.3 Elements of a Service Portfolio and Service Catalogue [Source: OGC ITIL Service Strategy ISBN 978-0-113310-45-6]

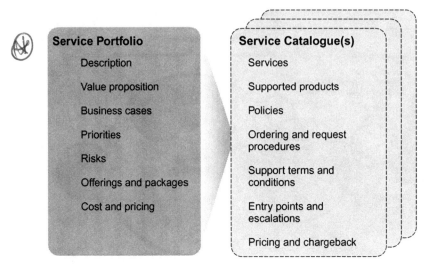

- **Analysed:** the set of requirements for the new service are being analysed and prioritised;
- **Approved:** the set of requirements for the new service have been finalised and authorised;
- **Chartered:** the new service requirements are being communicated and resources and budgets allocated;
- **Designed:** the new service and its constituent components are being designed (and procured, if required);
- **Developed:** the service and its constituent components are being developed or harvested, if applicable;
- **Built:** the service and its constituent components are being built;
- **Test:** the service and its constituent components are being tested;
- **Released:** the service and its constituent components are being released;
- **Operational:** the service and its constituent components are operational within the live environment;
- **Retired:** the service and its constituent components have been retired.

As a Service moves through its lifecycle, it moves from the Service Pipeline into the Service Catalogue once it has reached 'chartered' status and it is subsequently removed from the Service Catalogue once it has been 'retired'. However, it remains within the Service Portfolio at all stages of its lifecycle (see Figure 4.4).

Figure 4.4 The Service Portfolio and its contents (Source: OGC ITIL Service Design ISBN 978-0-113310-47-0)

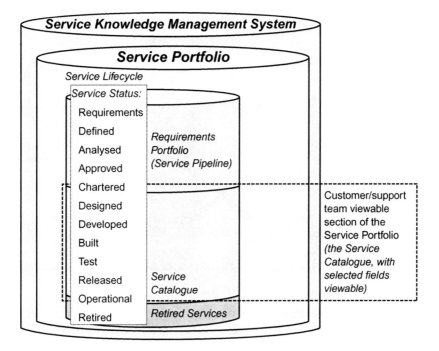

Ideally the Service Portfolio should form part of a comprehensive Service Knowledge Management System (SKMS) as shown in Figure 4.4. In most organisations the customers would only be able to view the Service Catalogue section of the Service Portfolio.

SYLLABUS REFERENCE: ITILMD03-3

Define and explain the Service Portfolio.

THE ROLE OF IT GOVERNANCE ACROSS THE SERVICE LIFECYCLE

Governance influences numerous areas of many organisations, including IT service providers of all types. Enterprise governance is a commonly used term that describes a framework covering corporate governance and business governance with an organisation (see Figure 4.5).

Enterprise governance considers the whole picture to ensure that strategic goals are aligned and good management is achieved.

Figure 4.5 Enterprise governance (Source: OGC ITIL Continual Service Improvement ISBN 978-0-113310-49-4)

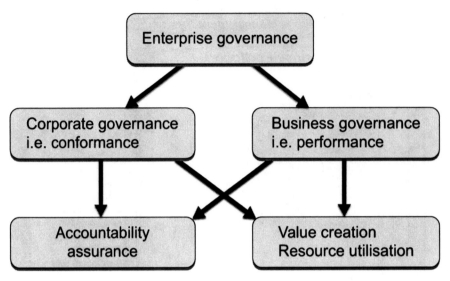

More recently, greater emphasis has been placed on corporate governance, which has led to greater pressure being exerted on service provider organisations for good governance.

'IT Governance is the responsibility of the board of directors and executive management. It is an integral part of enterprise governance and consists of the leadership, organisational structures and processes that ensure that the organisation's IT sustains and extends the organisation's strategies and objectives.' (Board Briefing on IT Governance, 2nd Edition, 2003, IT Governance Institute – ITGI)

IT service providers have to continually comply with new rules and legislation demonstrating their compliance through independent audits, while increasingly being required to deliver more with less and create additional value while maximising the use of existing resources. This continual and unceasing drive toward greater business value with greater internal efficiency is at the heart of Continual Service Improvement.

SYLLABUS REFERENCE: ITILMD03-4

Define and explain the role of IT Governance across the Service Lifecycle.

BUSINESS CASES

A Business Case is a decision support and planning tool that projects the likely consequences of a business action. The consequences can take on qualitative and quantitative dimensions. A financial analysis, for example, is frequently central to a good Business Case. The structure of a Business Case varies from organisation to organisation. Table 4.2 gives an example of the structure and content.

Table 4.2 Example Business Case structure

Section	Contents
1 Introduction	Presents the business objectives addressed by the service.
2 Methods and assumptions	Defines the boundaries of the Business Case, such as the time period, cost ownership and who benefits.
3 Business impacts	The financial and non-financial Business Case results.
4 Risks and contingencies	The probability that alternative results will emerge.
5 Recommendations	Specific actions recommended.

All business cases have a detailed analysis of the business impacts and benefits. The following questions are often asked within a Business Case, and addressed from a business and IT perspective. Not understanding some of the following questions can lead to challenges, perceived poor service or in some cases actual poor service.

- **Where are we now?** This is a question every business should ask because this creates a baseline of data for services currently being delivered.
- **What do we want?** This is often expressed in terms of business requirements such as 100 per cent availability.
- **What do we actually need?** When Service Level Management starts talking with the business they may realise they don't really need 100 per cent availability 24/7.
- **What can we afford?** This question often moves the business from looking at what they want to what they actually need.
- **What will we get?** This is often defined in an SLA for the service as well as service levels.

The Business Case should also consider the outcomes of the business action in terms of:

- **Improvements:** what is the outcome of the action in measurable terms: increase in a desirable metric or a decrease in an undesirable metric? (This could include both financial and non-financial benefits, such as a reduced risk of failure or reduction in the price of a transaction.)

- **Benefits:** the business gains and benefits from the actions and improvements. (This could again include both financial and non-financial benefits, such as a reduced time to market or reduced service costs.)

- **Return on investment (ROI):** the difference between the amount of expenditure and the benefit or saving in financial terms.

- **Value on investment (VOI):** the extra value created by the benefits, including non-monetary or long-term outcomes. ROI is a sub-component of VOI.

SYLLABUS REFERENCE: ITILMD03-5

Define and explain Business Cases.

SERVICE MODELS

Service Models are determined and influenced by many different factors as shown in Figure 4.6.

Figure 4.6 Service Models, Market Spaces, structure and dynamics (Source: OGC ITIL Service Strategy ISBN 978-0-113310-45-6)

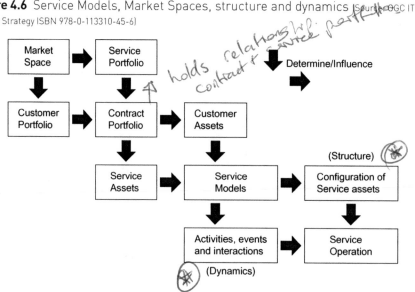

Service Models codify the strategy for a Market Space. They are blueprints for Service Management processes and activities to communicate and collaborate on value creation. Service Models show how Service Assets and customer assets interact to create value for a given portfolio of contracts and influence the structure and dynamics of the service. The structure and dynamics of the service have consequences for its subsequent design, transition and operation.

An IT service facilitates or enables a set of business processes by delivering the required business outcomes. It is important that the composition of the service and its components and relationships with other services, as shown in Figure 4.7, is understood.

Figure 4.7 Service components, relationships and dependencies (Source: OGC ITIL Service Design ISBN 978-0-113310-47-0)

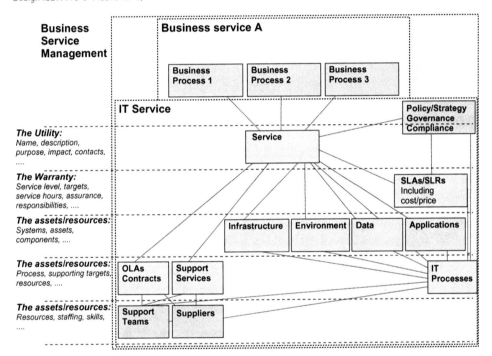

- **Service:** the service that is delivering value to the customers and the business.

- **SLA:** the document(s) agreed with the customers, defining the service levels, scope and quality of service to be delivered.

- **Infrastructure:** the IT equipment required to deliver the service to the customers and users.

- **Environment:** the facility and environmental equipment required to provide the physical location and security for the infrastructure.

- **Data:** the data and information necessary to meet the requirements of the business.

- **Applications:** the software required to process the data and provide the required business functionality.

- **Supporting services:** any additional services required to support the operation of the delivered services.

- **OLAs and contracts:** any underpinning agreements necessary to provide the required level of service delivered.

- **Support teams:** any internal team required to provide second- or third-line support for any of the required service components.

- **Suppliers:** any external organisation required to provide third- or fourth-line support for any of the required service components.

SYLLABUS REFERENCE: ITILMD03-6

Define and explain the Service Model.

 ## SERVICE DESIGN PACKAGES

A formal and structured approach to the design of a new or changed service is needed to ensure that the new service is of the right quality and functionality, and is within the right cost and time frame. The Service Design Package (SDP) contains everything required to take the new service solution through the remaining stages of its Lifecycle. An SDP should be produced during the design stage for each new service or major change to a service or retirement of a service. The SDP then passes from Service Design, through Service Transition, to Service Operation and Improvement, and contains everything necessary to manage the service through each of these stages. The SDP contains:

- **Requirements:** business requirements, service usage and applicability and service contacts.

- **Service Design:** service functional requirements, the SLR or new SLA, including service and quality targets, the service and operational management requirements and the service design and topology.

- **Organisational Readiness Assessment:** readiness assessment report and plan. This should include the business benefits of the new service solution, together with financial, technical, resource and organisational assessments, and details of the skills, competences and capabilities of the service provider and its suppliers.

- **Service Lifecycle Plan:** service programme, service transition plan, service operational plan and the Service Acceptance Criteria (SAC) and service acceptance plan.

CONFIGURATION MANAGEMENT SYSTEM

The effective support and management of complex IT services and infrastructure requires the use of a Configuration Management System (CMS).

CONFIGURATION MANAGEMENT SYSTEM

A Configuration Management System (CMS) is a set of tools and databases that are used to manage an IT service provider's configuration data. The CMS also includes information about Incidents, Problems, known errors, changes and releases, and may contain data about employees, suppliers, locations, Business Units, customers and users. The CMS includes tools for collecting, storing, managing, updating and presenting data about all Configuration Items and their relationships. The CMS is maintained by Configuration Management and is used by all IT Service Management Processes.

The CMS holds details and information for all Configuration Items (CIs) within the designated scope. The CMS maintains relationships between services and service components and any related Incidents, Problems, known errors, changes and releases as shown in Figure 4.8.

This diagram also shows the additional layers needed to provide the necessary integration, processing and presentation to enable easy access and retrieval of the information within the CMS.

THE SERVICE KNOWLEDGE MANAGEMENT SYSTEM (SKMS)

The ability to deliver a quality service depends on the knowledge of those involved and their ability to respond to circumstances and events. This ability and knowledge is becoming more and more dependent on the quality and accuracy of the information being made available to those involved in the operation and maintenance of IT services. Within IT Service Management this information is contained within the Service Knowledge Management System (SKMS) (see Figure 4.9).

Figure 4.8 The Configuration Management System (CMS) [Source: OGC ITIL Service Transition ISBN 978-0-113310-48-7]

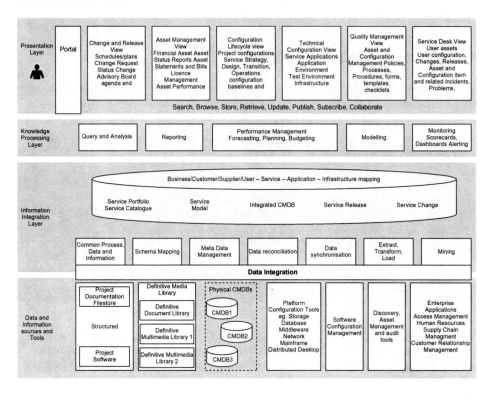

Figure 4.9 The relationship between the Configuration Management System, the Configuration Management Database and the Service Knowledge Management System [Source: OGC ITIL Service Transition ISBN 978-0-113310-48-7]

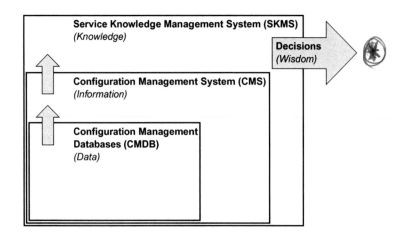

Figure 4.9 shows the three levels within the SKMS and the importance of both the Configuration Management System (CMS) and the Configuration Management Databases (CMDBs) within it. It is important to determine what data, information and knowledge is needed and how that information is stored, structured and accessed. It is essential that the system and information are easily accessible, otherwise the system will not be useful and will fall into decline. Therefore appropriate effort and consideration must be given to the structure and functionality provided by the presentation and knowledge processing layers in order to provide easy access to the knowledge and information (see Figure 4.10).

Figure 4.10 The Service Knowledge Management System (SKMS) (Source: OGC ITIL Service Transition ISBN 978-0-113310-48-7)

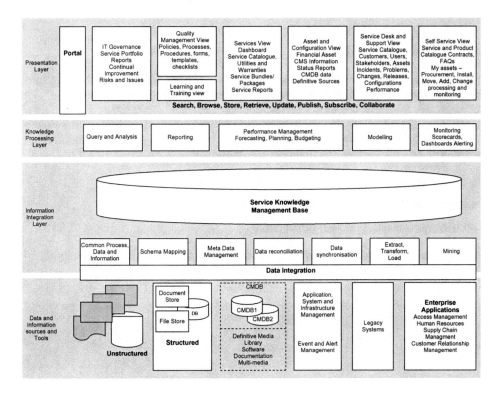

SYLLABUS REFERENCE: ITILMD03-8

Define and explain the Service Knowledge Management System (SKMS).

THE ROLE OF COMMUNICATION IN SERVICE OPERATION

Good communication is needed with other IT teams and departments, with users and customers and between the Service Operation teams and departments themselves.

27

The importance of this communication cannot be underestimated and all communications should have an intended audience and a purpose or resultant action. These areas of communication should include:

- routine operational communication;
- communication between shifts;
- performance reporting;
- communication in projects;
- communication related to changes;
- communication related to exceptions;
- communication related to emergencies;
- training on new or customised processes and service designs;
- communication of strategy and design to Operation teams.

These communications can be conducted in any suitable medium and should be controlled by a simple, flexible policy appropriate to the organisation.

Another important method of communication is the organisation and conducting of meetings. All meetings should have an agreed purpose, frequency and attendance and should be appropriately scheduled and managed. They should include:

- operations meetings;
- departmental, group or team meetings;
- customer meetings where appropriate.

The records of all meetings should be produced and made available in a timely manner.

SYLLABUS REFERENCE: ITILMD03-10

Define and explain the role of communication in Service Operation.

THE RACI MODEL

The clear definition of roles and responsibilities is essential to the effective operation of IT organisations. The RACI model is beneficial in enabling decisions on the roles and responsibilities of people within an organisation and within processes. The acronym RACI comes from the four functional roles of:

- **Responsible:** the person(s) responsible for completing the activity;
- **Accountable:** the person accountable for the activity. (Note that only one person can be accountable for each activity.);

 EXPECT IN EXAM

- **Consulted:** the people who are consulted and whose opinions are sought;
- **Informed:** the person or people who are kept up to date with activity progress.

Occasionally an expanded version of the RACI model, RACI-VS, is also used, which includes two additional functional roles:

- **Verifies:** the person or people that check or verify the activity has been completed to accepted criteria;
- **Signs off:** the person or people who approve or sign-off the activity as complete.

Table 4.3 An example RACI model

	Service Level Manager	Availability Manager	IT Service Continuity Manager	Capacity Manager
Activity 1	AR	C	C	C
Activity 2	I	AR	I	
Activity 3	A	R	R	R
Activity 4	I	I	I	AR

The RACI chart in Table 4.3 shows the power of RACI modelling with the activities down the left-hand side and the roles within the organisation shown across the top. The functional roles within the activity are defined within each of the table cells. The RACI model should be used to clearly define and assign the functional roles required rather than leaving them to chance. Duplications and conflicts can then be avoided and decisions can be made quickly and effectively if roles and interfaces are allocated in advance.

SYLLABUS REFERENCE: ITILMD07-2

Understand and analyse the RACI model and explain its role in determining organisational structure.

RISK MANAGEMENT

Risk is the uncertainty of a future outcome, whether a positive opportunity or a negative threat.

RISK

A risk is a possible event that could cause harm or loss, or affect the ability to achieve objectives. A risk is measured by the probability of a threat, the vulnerability of the asset to that threat, and the impact it would have if it occurred.

Managing risk requires the identification and control of exposure to risk. Each organisation should make cost-effective use of a risk framework that has a series of well-defined steps (see Figure 4.11).

Figure 4.11 A generic framework for Risk Management (Source: OGC ITIL Service Strategy ISBN 978-0-113310-45-6)

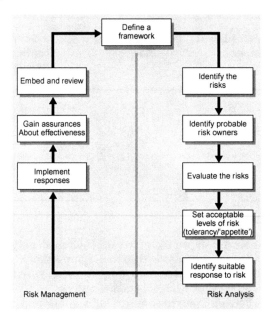

There are two distinct phases: Risk Analysis and Risk Management.

Risk Analysis is concerned with gathering information about exposure to risk so that the organisation can make appropriate decisions and manage risk appropriately. Risk Management involves having processes in place to monitor risks, access to reliable and up-to-date information about risks, the right balance of control in place to deal with those risks, and decision-making processes supported by a framework of Risk Analysis and evaluation.

SYLLABUS REFERENCE: ITILMD12-2

Define and explain Risk Management.

GENERIC ROLES

There are a number of generic roles required within the service management activities. Three of the key roles are Process Owner, Process Manager and Service Owner.

Process Owner

 PROCESS OWNER

A role responsible for ensuring that a process is fit for purpose. The Process Owner's responsibilities include sponsorship, design, change management and continual improvement of the Process and its metrics.

The main responsibilities of a Process Owner should include:

- documenting and publicising the Process;
- defining the Key Performance Indicators (KPIs) to evaluate the effectiveness and efficiency of the Process;
- reviewing KPIs and taking action required following the analysis;
- assisting with, and being ultimately responsible for, the Process design;
- improving the effectiveness and efficiency of the Process;
- providing input to the ongoing Service Improvement Plan (SIP);
- addressing any issues with the running of the Process;
- ensuring all relevant staff have the required training in the Process and are aware of their role in the Process;
- ensuring that the Process, roles, responsibilities and documentation are regularly reviewed and audited.

Process Manager

PROCESS MANAGER

A role responsible for operational management of a Process. The Process Manager's responsibilities include planning and co-ordination of all activities required to carry out, monitor and report on the Process.

The main responsibilities of a Process Manager should include:

- operational management of a Process;
- planning and coordination of all activities to carry out, monitor and report a Process.

The roles of Process Owner and Process Manager are often assigned to the same person, but they are usually separate in larger organisations where there may even be several Process Managers for one Process.

Service Owner

 SERVICE OWNER

A role which is accountable for the delivery of a specific IT Service.

The main responsibilities of a Service Owner should include:

- accountability for a specified service or Line of Service (LoS) through the entire Service Lifecycle;
- providing input into Service attributes such as performance, availability etc.;
- representing the Service across the organisation;
- understanding the Service Model and components etc.;
- being a point of escalation (notification) for major Incidents impacting the Service;
- representing the Service in Change Advisory Board meetings;
- providing input to Continual Service Improvement (CSI);
- participating in internal Service Review meetings (within IT);
- working with the CSI Manager to identify and prioritise service improvement;
- participating in external Service Review meetings (with the business);
- responsibility for ensuring that the service entry in the Service Catalogue is accurate and is maintained;
- participating in negotiating SLAs and OLAs associated with the Service.

SYLLABUS REFERENCE: ITILMD07-1

Understand and analyse the RACI model and explain its role in determining organisational structure.

5   SERVICE STRATEGY

LEARNING OBJECTIVES

The purpose of this chapter is to help candidates understand all aspects of the Service Strategy stage of the Lifecycle, including:

- the purpose, goals and objectives;
- the key concepts, definitions, principles and models;
- the Processes;
- the roles, responsibilities and functions.

Service Strategy provides useful advice and guidance for IT organisations in developing capabilities in Service Management. It also provides information on setting up and maintaining a strategic advantage in their goal of being a valuable service provider. It contains guidance on how to design, develop and implement Service Management both as an organisational capability and as a strategic asset to provide the basis of the core capabilities of service provision.

Strategic assets are carefully developed bundles of tangibles and intangibles, most notably knowledge, experience, systems and Processes. Service Management is a strategic asset because it constitutes the core capabilities for service providers and is effectively used for deploying Service Assets to provide services.

Service Strategy ensures that organisations can manage costs and risks associated with Service Portfolios and that they are organised not just for operational effectiveness, but for creating value and superior performance. Organisations should use the guidance to set goals and objectives, develop strategies for serving customers and expanding Market Spaces and to identify and prioritise opportunities.

PURPOSE, GOALS AND OBJECTIVES   — know for each of 5 stages

To operate and grow successfully in the long term, service providers must have the ability to think and act in a strategic manner. The purpose of the advice and guidance within the Service Strategy publication is to help organisations develop these abilities. The achievement of strategic goals or objectives requires the use of strategic assets. The guidance shows how to transform Service Management into a strategic asset by explaining the relationships between the services, systems and Processes that organisations manage and the Business Models, strategies or objectives they support. The guidance provides answers to the following kinds of question:

- What services should we offer and to whom?
- How do we differentiate ourselves from competing alternatives?
- How do we truly create value for our customers?
- How do we capture value for our stakeholders?
- How can we make a case for strategic investments?
- How can Financial Management provide visibility and control over value creation?
- How should we define service quality?
- How do we choose between different paths for improving service quality?
- How do we efficiently allocate resources across a portfolio of services?
- How do we resolve conflicting demands for shared resources?

A multi-disciplinary approach is required to answer questions such as these. Technical knowledge of IT is necessary but not sufficient. Knowledge of many additional disciplines such as operations management, marketing, finance, information systems, organisational development, systems dynamics and industrial engineering is also required. The result is a set of knowledge and guidance, robust enough to be appropriate and effective across a wide range of business environments.

Service Strategy provides guidance for IT organisations in developing capabilities in Service Management that set up and maintain a strategic advantage in the delivery of quality service provision. Service Strategy covers several aspects of Service Management including strategic objectives, providing direction for growth, prioritising investments and defining outcomes against which the effectiveness of Service Management may be measured. It is useful for influencing organisational attitudes and culture towards the creation of value for customers through the provision of IT services.

SYLLABUS REFERENCE: ITILMD02-3

Understand and explain the main goals and objectives of Service Strategy.

KEY CONCEPTS, DEFINITIONS, PRINCIPLES AND MODELS

The key principles and models described within this section are:

- Service Assets and Value Creation;
- value creation through services;
- service provider types;

- Service Structures;
- Service Strategy fundamentals.

Service Assets and Value Creation

Service Assets are used to create value for the customers of the service provider. Resources and Capabilities are Service Assets that organisations use to create value in terms of goods and services.

- **Resources** are the direct inputs used in the creation of services.

 - **Capabilities** are used to transform Resources and represent an organisation's ability to <u>coordinate, control and deploy</u> Resources to create value.

The use of these Resources and Capabilities are shown in Figure 5.1.

⊗ BUSINESS CREATES VALUE NOT IT.
↳ IT CREATES SERVICES

Figure 5.1 Business Units are coordinated goal-driven collections of assets
(Source: OGC ITIL Service Strategy ISBN 978-0-113310-45-6)

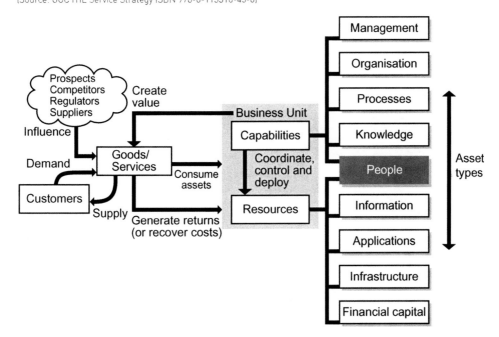

Capabilities are typically experience-driven, knowledge-intensive, information-based and firmly embedded within an organisation's people, systems, processes and technologies. It is relatively easier to acquire resources than capabilities.

SYLLABUS REFERENCE: ITILMD04-1

Explain how Service Assets are the basis of Value Creation.

Value Creation through services
The value of a service is influenced by what the customer:

- prefers (the preferences);
- perceives (the perceptions);
- gets (the business outcomes);
- values (the value) is frequently different from what the service provider delivers.

It is important therefore that service providers focus on delivering the business outcomes from the services and not solely on the Capabilities and Resources. The effective use of Service Assets to satisfy business outcomes through the delivery of IT services is the goal of every service provider. Service Assets should be used to increase the performance potential of services leading directly to an increase in the performance potential of customer assets delivering greater potential value through improved business outcomes. Wherever possible the constraints and the use of Service Assets should be pushed to the limit to maximise the value of the Service and the return on customer assets, as shown in Figure 5.2.

Figure 5.2 Customer assets are the basis for defining value 1 [Source: OGC ITIL Service Strategy ISBN 978-0-113310-45-6]

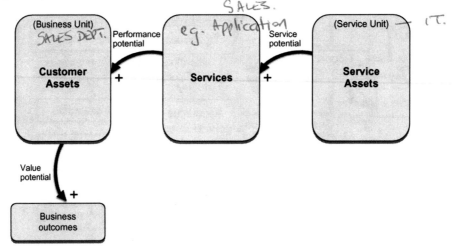

Customers can only obtain value from a Service which delivers on both the Utility (fit for purpose) and Warranty (fit for use). The Utility of a Service is the increase in potential gains from the performance of customer assets or the removal of constraints, leading to an increase in the probability of achieving business outcomes. Basically Utility increases the Service's performance average. Warranty is the decrease in potential losses for the customer from the variation in service performance. Warranty reduces the service's performance variation as shown in Figure 5.3.

Figure 5.3 Value of a Service in terms of returns on assets for the customer
(Source: OGC ITIL Service Strategy ISBN 978-0-113310-45-6)

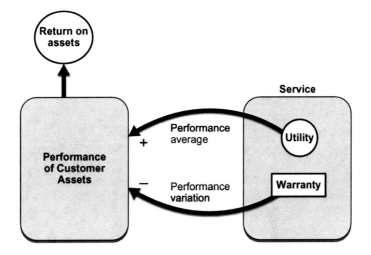

Bundling both core and supporting services within Service Packages enables differentiated offerings to be provided to customers.

 SERVICE PACKAGE

A detailed description of an IT service that is available to be delivered to customers. A Service Package includes a Service Level Package and one or more Core Services and Supporting Services.

 CORE SERVICE

An IT service that delivers basic outcomes desired by one or more customers.

 SUPPORTING SERVICE

A service that enables or enhances a Core Service. For example a Directory Service or a Backup Service.

By developing and offering services, either a Core Service or Supporting Services, with different levels of service, a service provider can provide a Line of Service (LoS) that meets the needs of different market segments.

LINE OF SERVICE (LOS)

A Core Service or Supporting Service that has multiple Service Level Packages. A Line of Service is managed by a Product Manager and each Service Level Package is designed to support a particular market segment.

Service Level Packages are associated with a set of service levels, pricing policies and a Core Service. Often organisations offer different levels of service in 'gold', 'silver' and 'bronze' level packages.

SERVICE LEVEL PACKAGE (SLP)

A defined level of Utility and Warranty for a particular Service Package. Each SLP is designed to meet the needs of a particular Pattern of Business Activity.

It is important that service providers recognise the importance of understanding and measuring Patterns of Business Activity (PBAs). If PBAs are understood then the capacity of the service can be predicted based on business forecasts and the Utility and Warranty of the services can be maintained.

PATTERN OF BUSINESS ACTIVITY

A workload profile of one or more business activities. Patterns of Business Activity are used to help the service provider understand and plan for different levels of business activity.

SYLLABUS REFERENCE: ITILMD04-2

Describe the basics of Value Creation through services.

Service provider types
Service providers can be divided into three different categories:

- **Type I:** internal service providers;
- **Type II:** shared services unit;
- **Type III:** external service providers.

Type I service providers are typically business functions embedded within the Business Units they serve. The Business Units themselves may be part of a larger enterprise (Figure 5.4).

Figure 5.4 Type I service providers (Source: OGC ITIL Service Strategy ISBN 978-0-113310-45-6)

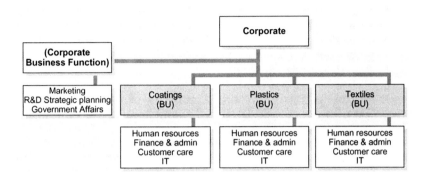

Type I service providers (internal service providers) have the benefit of close association with their customers, avoiding certain costs and risks. They specialise in, and provide, a narrow range of services focused on a small set of business needs, providing high levels of service and are therefore totally dependent on the success of the Business Unit they serve.

Type II service providers (internal service providers) provide services at a corporate level to many Business Units. The services of these shared functions are consolidated into an autonomous unit called a Shared Services Unit (SSU) (Figure 5.5).

Figure 5.5 Type II service providers (Source: OGC ITIL Service Strategy ISBN 978-0-113310-45-6)

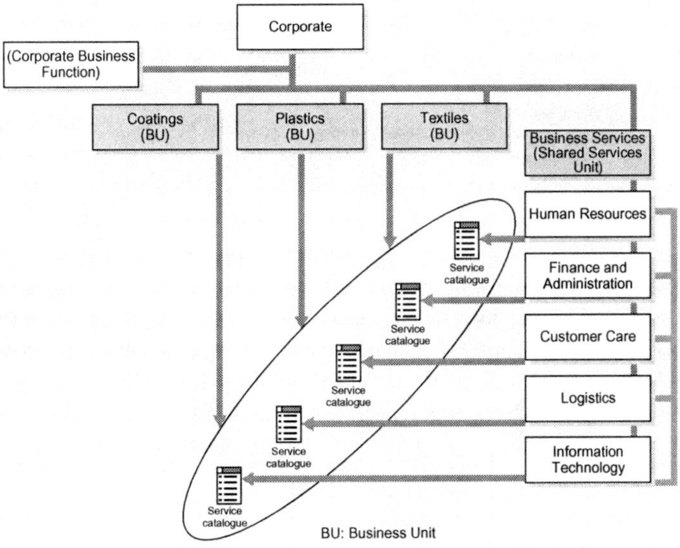

This model allows a more devolved governing structure under which the SSU can focus on serving Business Units as direct customers. An SSU can create, grow and sustain an internal market for their services and model themselves along the lines of service providers in the open market. They are, however, subject to comparisons with these external service providers and therefore need to compete with the performance of this type of provider. Type II service providers can offer economies of scale over Type I service providers and can often offer lower charges compared to Type III service providers.

Type III service providers (external service providers) can offer competitive prices and drive down unit costs by consolidating demand from a number of customers. Customers may pursue sourcing strategies requiring services from external providers. The motivation may be access to knowledge, experience, scale, scope, capabilities and resources that are beyond the reach of the business/customer organisation (Figure 5.6).

Figure 5.6 Type III service providers (Source: OGC ITIL Service Strategy ISBN 978-0-113310-45-6)

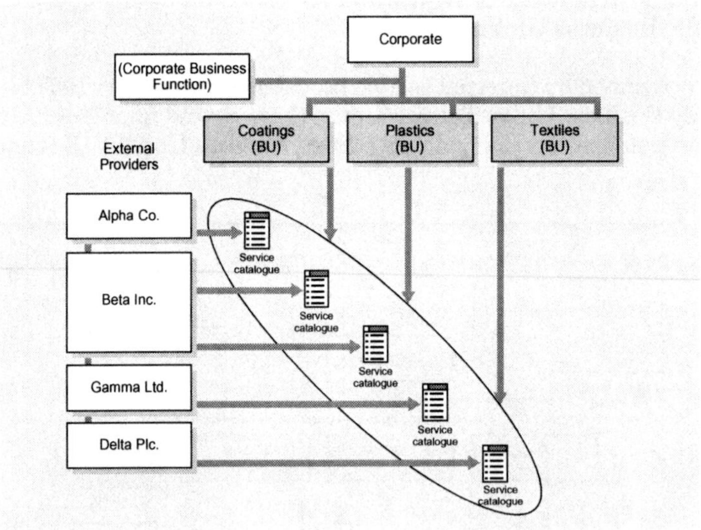

Market forces require organisations to have lean, flexible structures and in these situations it is often better to buy services from an external service provider, rather than own the assets and associated risks to execute particular business functions and processes. Type III providers are operating under an extended, larger scale shared services model. They assume a greater level of risk from their customers compared to Type I and Type II service providers, but their capabilities and resources are shared by their customers. The experience of Type III service providers is not necessarily limited to a single organisation or industry sector and therefore these organisations often have a greater breadth and depth of knowledge.

SYLLABUS REFERENCE: ITILMD04-3

Evaluate and explain Service Provider Types.

Service Structures

Customers pay service providers for the value they receive. This ensures that service providers make an adequate return on their assets. The relationship will remain good as long as the customer continues to receive value and the service provider continues to recover or exceed the costs incurred.

The process of creating value has been likened to an 'assembly line' and described as links in a value chain. Each Service provides value through a sequence of events and activities leading to the delivery and consumption of a Service. A service provider uses services from suppliers and adds value to those services by delivering new and enhanced services to their business and customers.

If we view service management as a set of 'collaborative exchanges', rather than an 'assembly line', the model for value creation changes. Service management can now be viewed more as a complex value network or value net rather than a simple value chain. (Figure 5.7).

Figure 5.7 Value network [Source: OGC ITIL Service Strategy ISBN 978-0-113310-45-6]

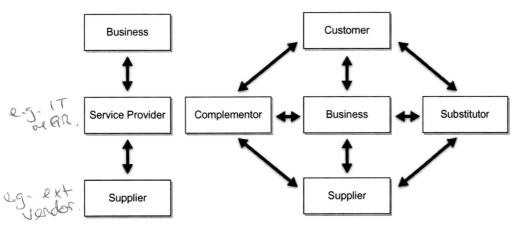

e.g. IT or HR.

e.g. ext vendor.

VALUE NETWORK — INSTEAD OF VALUE CHAIN

A value network is a web of relationships that generates tangible and intangible value through complex dynamic exchanges through two or more organisations.

Services are often characterised by complex networks of value flows often involving many parties that influence each other in many ways. Value nets illustrate this model in a clear and simple way (Figure 5.8).

 Figure 5.8 Basic value net (Source: OGC ITIL Service Strategy ISBN 978-0-113310-45-6)

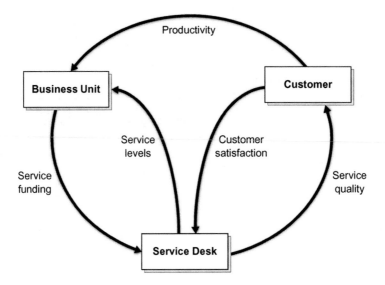

Each of the arrows in the diagram represents a transaction. The arrow indicates the direction of the transaction from the originator to the receiver. Transactions may be transient and may include either tangible or intangible deliverables. The following questions are useful in analysing the dynamics of a service model.

- Who are all the participants in the service?
- What are the overall patterns of exchange or transactions?
- What are the impacts or deliverables of each transaction on each participant?
- What is the best way to generate value?

SYLLABUS REFERENCE: ITILMD04-4

Understand and articulate Service Structures.

Service Strategy fundamentals

'The essence of strategy is choosing what not to do.' (Michael E Porter)

The value of services from a customer's perspective may change over time due to many conditions, events and factors outside a provider's control. A strategic view of Service Management means a carefully considered approach to the relationships with customers and a state of readiness in dealing with the uncertainties in the value that defines that relationship.

Successful strategies are based on the ability to take advantage of a set of distinct Capabilities in offering superior value to customers through services. Such Capabilities are viewed as strategic assets because a service provider can depend on them for success in a Market Space. Success comes from not only delivering value to customers but also being able to generate returns on investments. Strategic assets are carefully developed bundles of tangibles and intangibles, most notably knowledge, experience, systems and processes. Service Management is a strategic asset because it constitutes the core Capabilities for service providers. Service Management directs and controls service assets in effectively deploying them to provide services.

 The goal of a Service Strategy can be summarised as superior performance versus competing alternatives.

What distinguishes high-performing service providers is the manner in which they maintain superior performance. While many providers compete on the basis of a single point of differentiation, the competitive essence is almost always achieved through the balance, alignment and renewal of three building blocks:

 • **Market focus and position:** the emphasis is on developing Market Space. A Market Space is defined by a set of outcomes that customers desire, which can be supported by one or more services. High-performing service providers have remarkable clarity when identifying their Market Spaces and their Service offerings.

• **Distinctive Capabilities:** the emphasis is on creating and exploiting a set of distinctive, 'hard to replicate' Capabilities that deliver promised customer experience. This is about understanding the critical relationship between Resources and Capabilities and value creation and value capture. This ability is sometimes referred to as 'differentiation'.

 • **Performance anatomy:** the emphasis is on creating cultural and organisational characteristics that move service providers towards their goal of out-performing alternative suppliers, by establishing key principles such as:

  • services as strategic assets;

  • workforce productivity as a key differentiator;

  • continual improvement and renewal as real and permanent necessities.

The Lifecycle has at its centre Service Strategy. The starting point for strategy is referred to as the 'Four Ps of Strategy': Perspective, Position, Plan and Pattern. They identify the different forms a Service Strategy may take as shown by the example in Figure 5.9.

Figure 5.9 Strategic approach taken by a service provider (Source: OGC ITIL Service Strategy ISBN 978-0-113310-45-6)

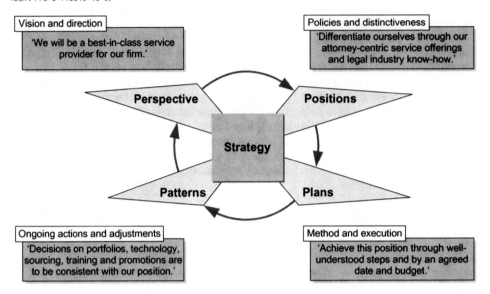

- **Perspective** describes a vision and direction. A strategic perspective articulates the business philosophy of interacting with the customer or the manner in which services are provided. It specifies a set of governing beliefs, values and a sense of purpose shared by the organisation.

- **Position** describes the decision to adopt a well defined-stance. Should the provider compete on the basis of:

  - value or low cost?
  - specialised or broad sets of services?
  - bias towards Utility or Warranty?

Positioning can be focused in terms of:

  - variety: focusing on providing a narrow set of services to many different types of customer;
  - needs: focusing on the requirements of a particular type of customer or industry sector;
  - access: focusing on providing services to customers with particular needs in terms of location, scale or structure;
  - a combination: focusing on a combination of positioning using more than one of the generic types of positioning.

- **Plan** describes the means of transitioning from the 'current state' to a 'future state'. How do we achieve and offer specialised services?

- **Pattern** describes a series of consistent decisions and actions over time. A service provider who continually offers dependable and reliable services is implementing a 'high-warranty' strategy.

SYLLABUS REFERENCE: ITILMD04-5

Compare and explain Service Strategy Fundamentals.

PROCESSES

The four main areas of activity within the Service Strategy stage of the Lifecycle are:

- define the market;
- develop the offerings;
- develop strategic assets;
- prepare for execution.

These four activities should be integrated with Financial Management to generate an appropriate strategy for the organisation. The Financial Management area of activity was contained in ITIL v2 and only the changes have been covered within this section.

Define the market
Defining the market consists of four related activities:

- services and strategy;
- understand the customer; + requirements
- understand the opportunities;
- classify and visualise the services.

Services and strategy
Organisations have an interest in strategy within the context of Service Management from two distinct but related perspectives:

- Strategies for services: where strategies are developed for services offered. The strategy is driven by the services.

- Services for strategies: where Service Management is a competence for offering services as part of a business strategy. By adopting a service-oriented approach the service provider can transform itself into a service business.

Understand the customer
Services are a means for managers to enable or enhance the performance of business assets leading to better outcomes. The value of a service is best

measured in terms of the improvement in outcomes that can be attributed to the impact of the service on the performance of business assets.

> ### KEY MESSAGE
>
> 'The performance of customer assets should be of primary concern to Service Management professionals because without customer assets there is no basis for defining the value of a service.'

The value of a service is always based on its ability to increase the performance of customer assets.

Understand the opportunities
It is important for managers to gain an insight into the business they serve. This includes identifying the outcomes for every customer and Market Space that is within the scope of their strategy. Customer outcomes that are not well supported represent opportunities to be explored and developed. Gaining an insight into the customer's business and having a good knowledge of customer outcomes is essential to the development of good business relationships with the customer. This is the purpose of Business Relationship Management (BRM).

Adopting an outcome-based definition of service ensures that all aspects of Service Management are planned and executed from the perspective of what is valuable to the customer. Such an approach ensures that services not only create value for customers, but also for the service provider.

Classify and visualise the services
Services differ primarily by the way they create value and in what context. Customer assets are the context in which value is created because they are linked to business outcomes that customers want to achieve.

- Customers own and operate different types of assets (a_n).
- Service providers offer different service archetypes/models offering specified and agreed Utility (u_n).

A combination of service archetype and customer assets $(u_n–a_n)$ represents an item in the Service Catalogue.

- Asset-based Service Strategy: Many service archetypes may be combined with the same type of customer asset (a_n).
- Utility-based Service Strategy: The same service archetype may be used to service different types of customer assets under a Utility-based Service Strategy.

These concepts are shown in Figure 5.10.

Figure 5.10 Asset-based and Utility-based positioning (Source: OGC ITIL Service Strategy ISBN 978-0-113310-45-6)

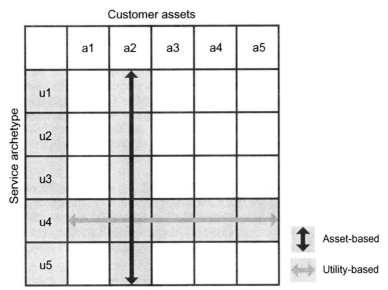

It is useful for managers to be able to visualise services as value-creating patterns of customer assets and service archetypes. Some combinations have more value for customers than others. Services with closely matching patterns are possible opportunities for consolidation or packaging as shared services.

A Service Strategy can result in a particular set of patterns (intended strategy) or a collection of patterns can make a particular strategy attractive (emergent strategy). This can be used as the basis for the development of a strategy for increasing the value of services and service assets.

Develop the offerings
Developing the offerings consists of three related activities:

- defining the Market Space;
- defining outcome-based services;
- managing the Service Pipeline and the Service Catalogue within the Service Portfolio.

Defining the Market Space
A Market Space is defined by a set of business outcomes, which can be facilitated by a service. A Market Space therefore represents a set of opportunities for service providers to deliver value to a customer's business through one or more services. This approach has definite value for service providers in building strong relationships with customers.

Defining outcome-based services

Unclear definitions of services lead to poor designs, ineffective operation and poor performance in service contracts. A well-formed definition of a service takes into account the context in which customers perceive value from the service and leads to effective and efficient Service Management processes.

An outcome-based definition of services ensures that all aspects of Service Management are viewed entirely from the perspective of what is of value to the customer. Being able to define services in an actionable manner has advantages from a strategic perspective. It removes ambiguity from decision-making and avoids 'the gap' between what the customer wants and what the service provider delivers. Service definitions are useful when they are broken down into discrete elements that can be assigned to different groups who can manage them to control the overall effect of delivering customer value.

Managing the Service Pipeline and the Service Catalogue within the Service Portfolio

The Service Portfolio represents the commitments and investments made by a service provider across all customers and Market Spaces. It represents present contractual commitments, new service developments and ongoing service improvements (see Figure 5.11).

Figure 5.11 Service Portfolio (Source: OGC ITIL Service Strategy ISBN 978-0-113310-45-6)

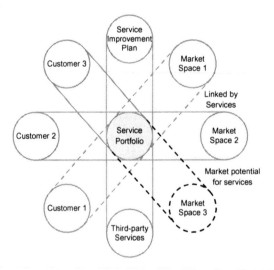

The Portfolio management approach helps managers prioritise investments and improve the allocation of Resources. Changes to Portfolios are governed by policies and procedures and Portfolios introduce the financial discipline necessary to avoid making inappropriate investments. Service Portfolios represent the ability and readiness of a service provider to serve customers and Market Spaces.

The Service Portfolio is divided into three areas as illustrated previously:

- The Service Pipeline (requirements and proposals).
- The Service Catalogue (live or being developed).
- The Retired Services (no longer required).

The Service Portfolio represents all the resources being used or released in various phases of the Service Lifecycle. The Service Portfolio should contain the right mix of services to ensure the financial viability of the service provider. Entry, progress and exit within the Service Portfolio are approved only with funding and a financial plan for recovering costs or showing profit as necessary. Service Portfolio Management (SPM) is about maximising value while managing risks and costs. The value realisation is derived from better service delivery and customer experiences. Through SPM, managers are better able to understand quality requirements and related delivery costs.

The Service Pipeline contains details of all of the services under development for a given Market Space or customer. These services are to be phased into operation by Service Transition once design, development and testing have been completed. The Pipeline represents the service provider's growth and strategic outlook for the future.

Approval is required from Service Transition to add or remove services from the Service Catalogue. The Service Catalogue is the only part of the Service Portfolio that recovers costs or earns a profit. Catalogue items are grouped into Lines of Service (LoS) based on the common Patterns of Business Activity (PBAs) they support.

Develop strategic assets
Service providers should treat Service Management as a strategic asset and entrust it with challenges and opportunities in terms of customers, services and contracts to support. Investments made in trusted assets are less risky because they have the capability to deliver consistently.

Customers perceive benefits in a continued relationship and entrust service providers with the business of increasing value and adding new customers and Market Spaces. This justifies further investment in Service Management in terms of Capabilities and Resources, which have a tendency to reinforce one another.

Stakeholders may initially trust the service provider with low-value contracts or non-critical services. If Service Management responds by delivering the performance expected of a strategic asset, they may be rewarded with contract renewals, new services and customers, which together represent a larger value of business. To handle this increase in value, Service Management must invest further in service assets such as process, knowledge, people, applications and infrastructure. Successful learning and growth enables commitments of higher service levels as Service Management capability develops. Over time, this virtuous cycle results in higher capability levels and maturity in Service Management leading to a higher return on assets for the service provider.

The development of strategic assets needs to consider two main areas:

- Service Management as a closed-loop control system;
- Service Management as a strategic asset.

Service Management as a closed-loop control system

As defined earlier, Service Management is a set of organisational capabilities specialised in providing value to customers in the form of services. The Capabilities interact with each other to function as a system for creating value. Service assets are the source of value and customer assets are the recipients (Figure 5.12).

 Figure 5.12 Service Management as a closed-loop control system [Source: OGC ITIL Service Strategy ISBN 978-0-113310-45-6]

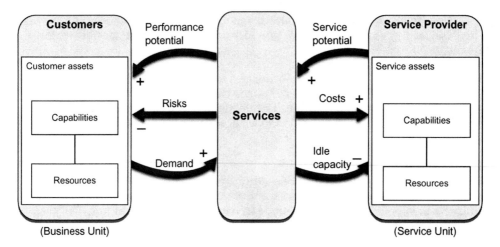

Services have the potential for increasing the performance of customer assets and creating value for the customer organisation. Improvements in the design, transition and operation of the service increase this customer performance potential and reduce the risks of variations on customer assets. This requires a comprehensive understanding of customer assets and desired outcomes.

Services derive their potential and value from service assets. Service potential is converted into performance potential of customer assets. Increasing the performance potential frequently stimulates additional demand for the service in terms of scale or scope. This demand translates into greater use of service assets, justification for their ongoing maintenance and upgrade and a reduction in unused capacity. From this perspective Service Management is a closed-loop control system. Costs incurred in fulfilling the demand should be recovered from the customer based on agreed terms and conditions.

Service Management as a strategic asset

In order to develop Service Management as a strategic asset, the value network within which the service provider operates in support of their customers must be defined. Often this value network extends across organisational boundaries with many other organisations being involved within the value network. By identifying the key relationships and interactions in the network, managers have better visibility and control over the services, systems and processes they operate. This allows managers to manage the complexity that exists in their business environments as customers pursue their own business models and strategies. It also helps account for all the costs and risks involved in providing a service or supporting a customer.

Increasing service potential The Capabilities and Resources (service assets) of a service provider represent the service potential or the productive capacity available to customers through a set of services. Projects that develop or improve Capabilities and Resources increase the service potential. One of the key objectives of Service Management is to improve the service potential of the Service Management Capabilities and Resources.

Through Service Asset and Configuration Management (SACM), the process responsible for both Configuration Management and Asset Management, all service assets should be tagged with the name of the services to which they add service potential. This helps decisions related to service improvement and asset management. SACM is a process similar to Configuration Management, but with the added responsibility for the management, protection and integrity of all service assets as well as Configuration Items (CIs). Clear relationships between service assets and CIs make it easier to ascertain the impact of changes, make business cases for investments in service assets, and identify opportunities for scale and scope economies. It also helps identify critical service assets across the Service Portfolio for a given customer or Market Space.

Increasing performance potential The services offered by a service provider represent the potential to increase the performance of customer assets. Service providers should visualise and define the performance potential of services so that decisions made by managers are based on the creation of value for customers. This approach avoids many of the problems of service businesses where value for customers is created in intangible forms and therefore are harder to define and control.

The 'performance potential' of services is increased primarily by having the right mix of services available to offer to customers. The key questions to be asked are:

- What is our Market Space?
- What does that Market Space want?
- Can we offer anything unique in that Market Space?
- Is the Market Space already saturated with good solutions?
- Do we have the right Portfolio of Services developed for a given Market Space?

- Do we have the right Catalogue of Services offered to a given customer?
- Is every service designed to support the required outcomes?
- Is every service operated to support the required outcomes?
- Do we have the right models and structures to be a service provider?

Demand, capacity and cost When services are effective in increasing the performance potential of customer assets there is often an increase in the demand for the services. This acts as a positive feedback to the system to be taken into account. An increase in the performance potential leads to an increase in customer demand.

As the maturity of Service Management increases, it is possible to deliver higher levels of Utility and Warranty without a proportional increase in costs. Due to the effect of fixed costs and overheads, the costs of providing additional units of service output can decrease with an increase in the demand for services and the economies of scale.

Prepare for execution

An appropriate Service Strategy should be developed for each service provider organisation. Strategy involves both thinking and doing as shown in Figure 5.13.

Figure 5.13 Forming and formulating a strategy (Source: OGC ITIL Service Strategy ISBN 978-0-113310-45-6)

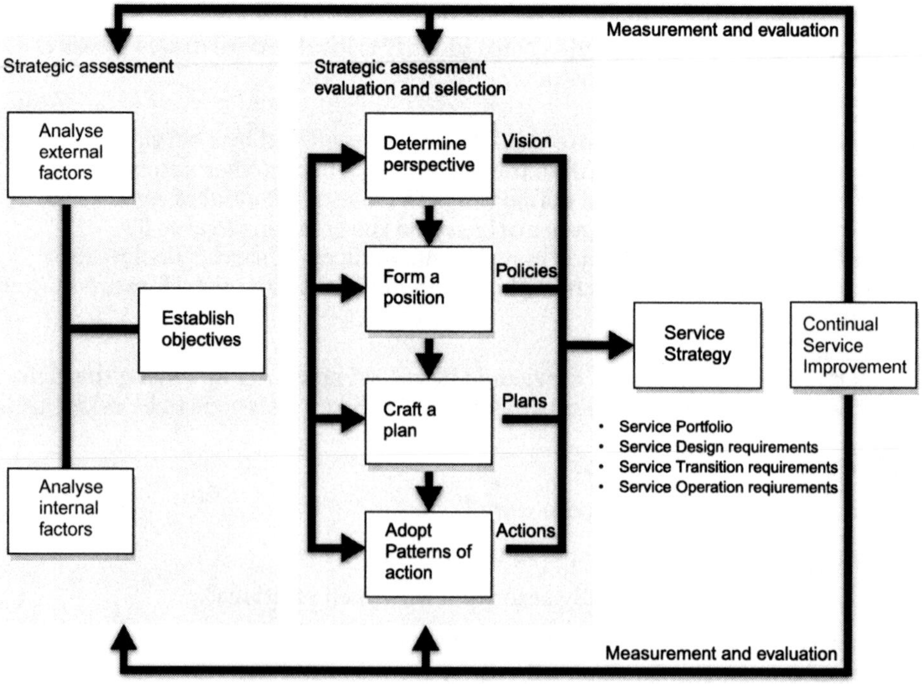

The Strategy should be developed through reflection and analysis to be suitable within the context and situation of the organisation. Strategy is critical to the performance of the organisation.

Strategic assessment

In developing a Service Strategy, a provider should first take a careful look at what it does already. It is likely that a core of differentiation from other service providers already exists. An established service provider frequently lacks an understanding of its own unique differentiators. In order to address this shortfall, an assessment of the internal and external influencing factors should be completed including:

- strengths and weaknesses;
- distinctive competencies;
- business strategy;
- critical success factors;
- threats and opportunities.

Answers to the following questions can also help a service provider clarify their distinctive differentiators and capabilities:

- Which of our services are the most distinctive?
- Which of our services are the most profitable?
- Which of our customers and stakeholders are the most satisfied?
- Which customer channels or purchase occasions are the most profitable?
- Which of our activities in our value chain or value network are the most different and effective?

Objectives can then be based on the findings from the results of the assessment or the answers to the questions. Objectives are expected results and strategies are actions. Clear objectives result in consistent decision-making, thereby minimising later conflicts. They also set priorities and serve as guidelines and standards.

In order to define its objectives, an organisation must understand what outcomes customers desire to achieve and determine how best to satisfy the important outcomes currently underserved. This is how metrics are determined for measuring how well a service is performing. The objectives for a service include three distinct types of data. These data sources are the primary means by which a service provider creates value:

- **Customer tasks:** what activity is the service required to carry out?
- **Customer outcomes:** what outcomes does the customer require?
- **Customer constraints:** what constraints may inhibit the desired outcomes?

There are four common categories of information that are often gathered and presented as objectives:

- **Solutions:** customers present their requirements in the form of a solution to a problem.

- **Specifications:** customers present their requirements in the form of specifications.

- **Needs:** customers present their requirements as high-level descriptions of the overall quality of service.

- **Benefits:** customers present their requirements in the form of benefits' statements.

Strategic assessment, evaluation and selection

The model shown in Figure 5.13 represents a clear and practical approach for producing an effective Service Strategy based on the 'Four Ps of Strategy' discussed earlier.

- **Determine Perspective:** develop and document the vision and direction for the organisation, providing a purpose, and a set of governing beliefs and values.

- **Form a Position:** develop policies focused on the appropriate set of services to meet the needs of the identified customers.

- **Craft a Plan:** develop plans to move from the 'current state' to the agreed desired 'future state'.

- **Adopt Patterns of action:** adopt a set of consistent decisions and actions to achieve the agreed objectives.

Aligning service assets with customer outcomes

Service providers must manage assets in a similar way to their customers. Service assets should be coordinated, controlled and deployed in a manner that maximises the value to customers while minimising risks and costs for the provider.

Defining critical success factors

For every Market Space there are Critical Success Factors (CSFs) that determine the success or failure of a Service Strategy. These factors are influenced by customer needs, business trends, competition, regulatory environment, suppliers, standards, industry best practices and technologies. CSFs have the following general characteristics:

- They are defined in terms of Capabilities and Resources.

- They are proven to be key determinants of success by industry leaders.

- They are defined by Market Space levels; they are not peculiar to any one organisation.

- They are the basis for competition among rivals.

- They change over time, so they are dynamic not static.

- They usually require significant investments and time.

- Their value is extracted by combination with other factors.

Identifying CSFs for a Market Space is an essential aspect of strategic planning and development. Service providers in each Market Space require a core set of assets in order to support a set of customers or a Customer Portfolio through a Service Portfolio.

CUSTOMER PORTFOLIO

A database or structured document used to record all customers of the IT service provider. The Customer Portfolio is Business Relationship Management's view of the customers who receive services from the IT service provider.

Critical Success Factors and competitive analysis

Critical Success Factors (CSFs) are determinants of success in a Market Space. They are also useful in evaluating a service provider's strategic position in a Market Space and in driving changes to such positions. This requires CSFs to be further refined in terms of a distinct value proposition to customers.

A strategic analysis should be conducted for every Market Space, major customer and Service Portfolio to determine current strategic positions and desired strategic positions for success. This analysis requires service providers to gather data from customer surveys, Service Level Reviews, industry benchmarks and competitive analysis conducted by third parties or internal research teams. Each CSF should be measured on a meaningful index or scale. It is best to adopt indices and scales that are commonly used within a Market Space or industry to facilitate benchmarking and comparative analysis. CSFs are used to define playing fields, which serve as reference frameworks for evaluation of strategic positions and competitive scenarios (Figure 5.14).

Figure 5.14 Critical Success Factors and competitive positions in playing fields
(Source: OGC ITIL Service Strategy ISBN 978-0-113310-45-6)

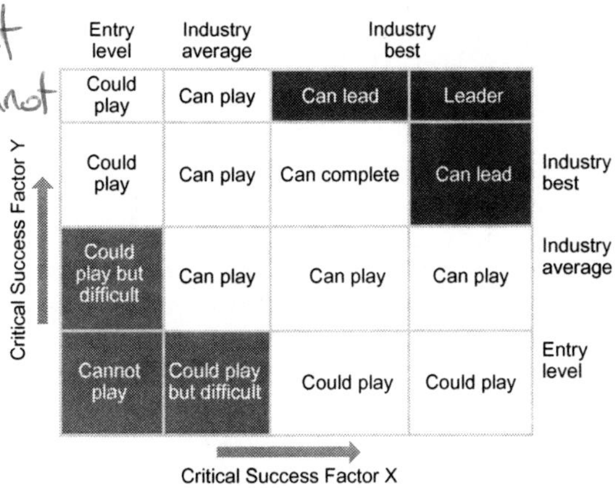

[Handwritten annotations:]
understand what you can + cannot do + focus
↳ competitive position

(*) Try to lead rather than being average.

Strategic analysis should take into account not only the current benchmarks for a playing field but also the direction in which they are expected to move (higher or lower), the magnitude of change and the related probabilities. This analysis is necessary for service providers to avoid being surprised by changes in the Market Space that can completely destroy their value proposition.

Prioritising investments

One common problem service providers have is prioritising investments and managerial attention on the right set of opportunities. There is a hierarchy in customer needs for individuals. At any one time, the business needs of customers are fulfilled to varying levels of satisfaction. The combination of hierarchy or importance of a need and its current level of satisfaction determines the priority in the customer's mind for purchases. The best opportunities for service providers lie in areas where an important customer need remains poorly satisfied.

Service Portfolios should be extended to support such areas of opportunity. This typically means there is a need for services to provide certain levels of Utility and Warranty. However, managers should not overlook the costs and risks in such areas. There are usually strong reasons why certain needs of customers remain unfulfilled.

Exploring business potential

Service providers can be present in several Market Spaces. As part of strategic planning and review, service providers should analyse their presence across Market Spaces, including the analysis of strengths, weaknesses, opportunities and threats in each Market Space. Service providers should also analyse their business potential based on unserved or underserved Market Spaces. The long-term vitality of the service provider rests on supporting customer needs as they change or grow as well as exploiting new opportunities that emerge. This analysis identifies opportunities with current and prospective customers. It also prioritises investments in service assets based on their potential to serve Market Spaces of interest.

Alignment with customer needs

Since Market Spaces are defined in terms of the business needs and outcomes desired by customers, the changes and adjustments are ultimately based on the dynamics of the customer's business environment. This is the most important reason why service providers must think in terms of Market Spaces and not simply industry sectors, geographies or technology platforms.

Once Service Strategies are linked to Market Spaces, it is easier to make decisions on Service Portfolios, designs, operations and long-term improvements. Investments in service assets such as skills' sets, knowledge, processes and infrastructure are driven by the CSFs for a given Market Space. The growth and expansion of any business is less risky when anchored by core capabilities and demonstrated performance. Successful expansion strategies are often based on leveraging existing service assets and Customer Portfolios to drive new growth and profitability.

Differentiation in Market Spaces

Services provide Utility to customers in a given Market Space by delivering benefit with a level of assurance (i.e. Warranty). Market Spaces can be defined anywhere an opportunity exists to improve the performance of customer assets. Service Strategy is about how to provide distinctive value in each Market Space. Service providers should analyse every Market Space they support and determine their position with respect to the options that customers have with other service providers.

SYLLABUS REFERENCE: ITILMD05-1

Understand and communicate the four main activities in the Service Strategy process.

Service Portfolio Management

SERVICE PORTFOLIO MANAGEMENT (SPM)

The process responsible for managing the Service Portfolio. Service Portfolio Management considers services in terms of the business value that they provide.

A Service Portfolio describes a service provider's services in terms of business value and articulates business needs and the service provider's response to those needs. The objective of Service Portfolio Management (SPM) is to provide a dynamic method for governing investments in Service Management across the enterprise and managing them for value.

A Service Portfolio helps clarify the answers to the following strategic questions by acting as the basis of a decision-making framework:

- Why should a customer buy these services?
- Why should they buy these services from us?
- What are the pricing or chargeback models?
- What are our strengths and weaknesses, priorities and risk?
- How should our Resources and Capabilities be allocated?

The scope of the SPM process should cover all of the services, in all stages of their Lifecycle within the Service Pipeline, the Service Catalogue and also the Retired Services.

The value of a Service Portfolio strategy is demonstrated through the ability to anticipate change while maintaining traceability to strategy and planning. SPM is a dynamic method for governing investments in Service Management across the enterprise and managing them for value.

A portfolio is essentially a group of investments that share similar characteristics. They are grouped by size, discipline or strategic value. There are few fundamental differences between SPM and Project Portfolio Management. They are both techniques for enabling governance.

The SPM process consists of four steps as shown in Figure 5.15.

Figure 5.15 The Service Portfolio Management process (Source: OGC ITIL Service Strategy ISBN 978-0-113310-45-6)

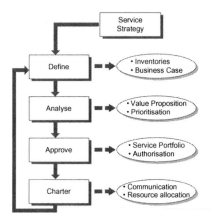

Define: inventory services, ensure business cases and validate portfolio data

This step consists of collecting an inventory containing information on every existing or proposed service. The cyclic nature of the SPM process means that this step of the process not only creates an initial inventory of services, but also validates the information on a regular basis. Every service in the Service Portfolio should include a Business Case, which is a model of what the service is expected to achieve. It is the assessment of the service investment in terms of the potential benefits and the Resources and Capabilities required to deliver and maintain the service.

Analyse: maximise Portfolio value, align and prioritise and balance supply and demand

The strategic intent within this step is crafted with a set of questions:

- What are the long-term goals of the service provider organisation?

- What services are required to meet those goals?

- What Capabilities and Resources are required for the organisation to be able to deliver those services?

- How will we get there?

In other words, what are the perspective, position, plan and the patterns? The answers to these questions guide not only the analysis, but also the desired outcomes of SPM.

Approve: finalise proposed portfolio, authorise services and resources
The previous steps have led to a well-understood future 'to be' state. This is where the deliberate approval or non-approval of the future state takes place. The authorisation of new services and Resources comes with the approval. The outcomes for existing services fall into one of six categories:

- **Retain:** these services are aligned with and are relevant to the organisation's strategy and will continue to be provided.

- **Replace:** these services have unclear and overlapping functionality and will be superseded by other services.

- **Rationalise:** reduce the number of variations within services where multiple versions of software/platform are used to provide similar functions. A reduced set of standardised services will be provided.

- **Refactor:** these technical services often provide 'fuzzy' Processes or system boundaries. These should be refactored to include only the core functionality with common services used to provide the remainder.

- **Renew:** these services meet functional fitness requirements, but fail technical fitness and are therefore renewed by using newer technology.

- **Retire:** these services do not meet minimum levels of functional and technical fitness and will be removed.

Charter: communicate decisions, allocate resources and charter services
The decisions and actions from the 'approve' step are communicated to the organisation and are correlated with budgetary decisions and financial plans. The Resources are allocated and the expected value of each service is built into financial forecasts. Newly chartered services are referred to Service Design, existing services are refreshed by Service Design and retired services are transferred to Service Transition.

The Option Space tool
A useful tool for making decisions on the timing and sequencing of investments within the Service Portfolio is called the Option Space tool (see Figure 5.16).

An Option Space can guide decisions to invest and, if so, when. The Value-to-Cost axis represents the ratio of a service's worth to its cost. A Value-to-Cost of less than one designates a service worth less than what it costs. When the measure is greater than one, the present value of the service is greater than its cost and is a

Figure 5.16 Option Space: focused on maintaining services (Run The Business (RTB))
[Source: OGC ITIL Service Strategy ISBN 978-0-113310-45-6]

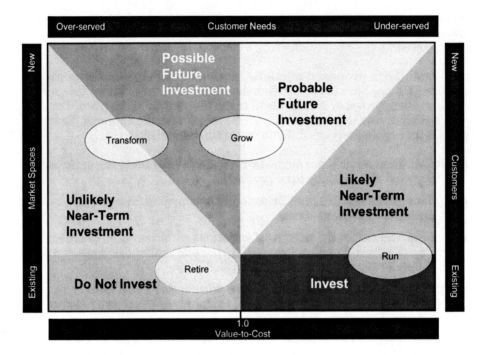

more likely option for future investment. Financial measures, however, need not be the only measure. Other factors can and should be incorporated such as:

- mission imperatives;
- compliance;
- trends;
- intangible benefits;
- strategic or business fit;
- social responsibilities;
- innovation.

The other axes are based on Market Spaces, customers and customer needs, and each is used as a guide for strategic intent.

Senior executives have constraints and limited resources. They must understand the risks, impacts and dependencies that exist within the organisation. Understanding these relationships will allow them to make informed investments in service initiatives with the appropriate levels of risk and reward.

Service investments are split between three strategic categories, which are further divided into the budget allocations as shown in Figure 5.17.

 Figure 5.17 Investment categories and budget allocations (Source: OGC ITIL Service Strategy ISBN 978-0-113310-45-6)

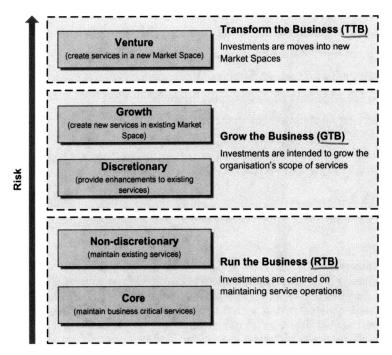

By determining the allocation of budget into 'Run The Business' (RTB), 'Grow The Business' (GTB) or 'Transform The Business' (TTB) service categories, executives are not only affirming their risk tolerance on SPM, but are directly affecting the modes of operations implemented by the operational staff. The distribution of services from RTB to TTB will reflect the nature of the organisation:

- predominantly RTB, if IT is a cost centre (back-office) (an example of this is shown in Figure 5.16);
- predominantly TTB, if IT is an investment centre (commercial provider).

The Key Performance Indicators and the challenges
Some of the main Key Performance Indicators (KPIs) of the SPM process that should be considered for measuring the effectiveness of the process are:

- the accuracy of the data within the Service Portfolio;
- the value-to-cost ratio of services;

- the percentage of Business Cases realising their full business benefits;
- the percentage of decisions made without appropriate or accurate data available within the Service Portfolio.

The challenges facing the SPM process are:

- meeting the needs and expectations of the customers and the business;
- gaining appropriate support and commitment to the Service Portfolio;
- gaining appropriate involvement of key business personnel;
- the availability and access to the overall organisational strategy;
- the availability of service assets and financial budget;
- maintaining an accurate Service Portfolio.

SYLLABUS REFERENCE: ITILMD05-2a

Explain the objectives, scope, concepts, activities, key metrics, roles and challenges for Service Portfolio Management.

Demand Management

Demand Management is a critical aspect of Service Management. Poorly managed demand is a source of risk for service providers because of uncertainty in demand. Excess capacity generates cost without creating value. The objective of Demand Management should therefore be to provide the appropriate level of service capacity in all areas of IT to meet the current and future agreed business demands.

The scope of the Demand Management process should include the capacity and performance of all service assets and the associated customer assets and should include the following Process activities:

- Identify, analyse and record Patterns of Business Activity (PBA).
- Define and record Lines of Service (LoS).
- Define and develop User Profiles (UPs).
- Identify and categorise core and supporting services.
- Develop differentiated service offerings.
- Define and record Service Level Packages (SLPs).
- Understand the relationship between business Processes and activities, PBAs, demand and service performance and capacity.

These concepts and activities are explained within this section on Demand Management.

Business activities drive demand for services. Customer assets, such as people, Processes and Resources, generate patterns of business activity (PBA). PBA define the dynamics of a business and include interactions with customers, suppliers, partners and other stakeholders. Services often directly support PBA. Since PBA generate revenue, income and costs they account for a large proportion of business outcomes.

PBA are identified, codified and shared across Processes for clarity and completeness of detail. One or more attributes such as frequency, volume, location and duration describe business activity. They are associated with requirements such as security, privacy and latency or tolerance for delays. This profile of business activity can change over time with changes and improvements in business Processes, people, organisation, applications and infrastructure.

A User Profile (UP) is a pattern of user demand for services. Each UP includes one or more PBA. UPs are based on roles and responsibilities within organisations for people, and on functions and operations for Processes and applications. Often business Processes are treated as users in many business contexts. Many Processes are not actively executed or controlled by staff or personnel. Process automation allows for Processes to consume services on their own. Processes can have UPs. Whether they should is a matter of judgement. Each UP can be associated with one or more PBA.

The Service Catalogue is a visualisation tool for SPM decisions. In the Catalogue, demand for services comes together with the capacity to fulfil demand. Customer assets attached to a business outcome are sources of demand (Figure 5.18).

Figure 5.18 Demand Management and the Service Catalogue (Source: OGC ITIL Service Strategy ISBN 978-0-113310-45-6)

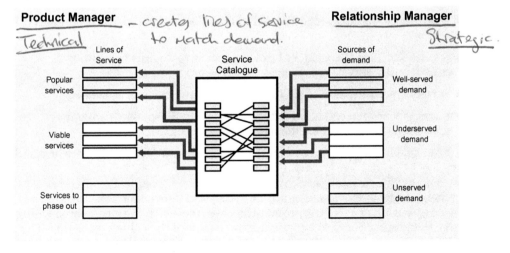

In particular, customers have expectations of services Utility and Warranty. If any items in the Catalogue can fulfil those expectations, connections are made resulting in service contracts or agreements. Catalogue items are clustered into Lines of Service (LoS) based on the common PBA they can support.

Lines of Service (LoS) performing well are allocated additional resources to ensure continued performance and anticipate increases in demand. Items performing above a financial threshold are deemed viable services. An effort is to be made to make them popular by introducing new attributes, new SLPs, improved matches with sources of demand or by new pricing policies. If performance drops below a threshold, then the services are marked for retirement. A new Service Transition project is initiated to phase out the service.

Demand Management techniques, such as off-peak pricing, differential charging, volume discounts and differentiated service levels can influence the arrival and pattern of demand. Demand and capacity are more tightly coupled in the service industry than in product-related industries. Some types of capacity can be quickly increased as required and released when not in use. Others have a long lead time for implementation and release.

Activity-based Demand Management recognises that business processes and activities are the primary source of demand for services. PBA influence the demand patterns seen by the service providers. It is very important to study the customer's business to identify, analyse and codify such patterns to provide sufficient basis for Capacity Management. It is then possible to visualise the customer's business activity and plans in terms of the demand for supporting services.

Some of the benefits for analysing PBA are in the form of inputs to Service Management functions and processes such as the following:

- Service Design can then optimise designs to suit demand patterns.
- The Service Catalogue can be used to map demand patterns to appropriate services.
- Service Portfolio Management can approve investments in additional capacity, new services or changes to services.
- Service Operation can adjust allocation of Resources and scheduling.
- Service Operation can identify opportunities to consolidate demand by grouping closely matching demand patterns.
- Financial Management can approve suitable incentives to influence demand.

Developing differentiated service offerings can be achieved by bundling services together to increase customer value. Core Services deliver the basic outcomes desired by customers. They represent the value for which the customer is willing to pay. Supporting Services either enable or enhance the value proposition. The packaging of Core and Supporting Services is an essential element of marketing strategy. The decisions are invariably strategic for the service provider because they provide a long-term plan for maintaining value for customers. Bundling of support services has implications for the design and operation of services.

Services packages come with one or more Service Level Packages (SLPs). Each SLP provides a definite level of Utility or Warranty from the perspective of outcomes, assets and the PBA of customers. Each SLP is capable of fulfilling one or more patterns of demand. SLPs are associated with a set of service levels, pricing policies and a core service package (CSP). CSPs are service packages that provide a platform of Utility and Warranty shared by two or more SLPs as shown in Figure 5.19.

Figure 5.19 Service Level Packages are a means to provide differentiated services
(Source: OGC ITIL Service Strategy ISBN 978-0-113310-45-6)

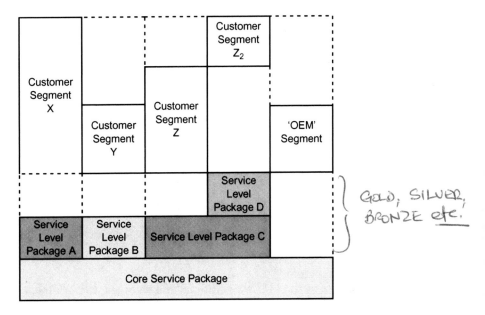

Combinations of CSPs and SLPs are used to serve customer segments with differentiated value. Common attributes of SLPs are subsumed into the supporting CSPs. This follows the principle of modularity to reduce complexity, increase asset utilisation across SLPs, and to reduce the overall cost of services. CSPs and SLPs are loosely coupled to allow for local optimisation while maintaining efficiency over the entire supported Service Catalogue. Improvements made to CSPs are automatically available to all SLPs following the principle of inheritance. Economy of scale and economy of scope are realised at the CSP level and the savings are transmitted to the SLP and to customers as policy permits.

Some enterprises have highly consolidated core infrastructure units that support the operations of Business Units at a very large scale with high levels of reliability and performance. SLPs are effective in developing Service Packages for providing value to a segment of users with Utility and Warranty appropriate to their needs and in a cost-effective way.

Some of the main KPIs of the Demand Management process that should be considered for measuring the effectiveness of the process are:

- the number of service level breaches caused by unpredicted demand within the monitoring period;
- the level/number/size of unused or wasted service capacity;
- the use/volume of differentiated service offerings and SLPs.

The challenges facing the Demand Management process are:

- gaining appropriate involvement of key business personnel and activities;
- avoiding the cost of excess unwanted capacity;
- avoiding a lack of capacity causing the breach of agreed service levels;
- predicting demand for services;
- agility in responding to changes in demand;
- synchronous production and consumption: unused service capacity cannot be stacked or stored.

SYLLABUS REFERENCE: ITILMD05-2a

Explain the objectives, scope, concepts, activities, key metrics, roles and challenges for Demand Management.

Financial Management

This section covers the ITIL v3 additions and changes within Financial Management. The purpose of Financial Management is to provide the business and IT with the quantification, in financial terms, of the value of IT services, the value of the assets underlying the provisioning of those services and the qualification of operational forecasting.

The objectives of Financial Management are:

- to provide operational visibility, insight and superior decision-making;
- to provide quantification of the costs and value of services and service components;
- to provide comprehensive financial information to aid informed decision-making;
- to assist Service Portfolio Management by providing knowledge and analysis in order to assess the expected value and/or return of a given initiative, solution, programme or project;
- to provide appropriate financial compliance and control.

The scope of the Financial Management process is to assist IT and the business to identify, document and agree the costs and value of the services being delivered and to enable Service Demand modelling and Management.

The main additions to Financial Management are:

- service valuation;
- planning confidence;
- service investment analysis;
- methods, models, activities and techniques.

Service valuation

Service valuation quantifies, in financial terms, the funding required by the business and IT for services delivered, based on the agreed value of those services. Financial Management calculates and assigns a monetary value to a service or service component so that they may be disseminated across the enterprise once the business customer and IT identify what services are actually desired.

The pricing of a service is the cost-to-value translation necessary to achieve clarity and influence the demand and consumption of services. The activity involves identifying the cost baseline for services and then quantifying the perceived value added by a provider's service assets in order to conclude a final service value. The primary goal of service valuation is to produce a value for services that the business perceives as fair, and fulfils the needs of the provider in terms of supporting it as an ongoing concern.

Within this definition, the service value elements of Warranty and Utility require translation of their value to an actual monetary figure. Therefore service valuation focuses primarily on two key valuation concepts: provisioning value and service value potential.

Provisioning value is the actual underlying cost to IT related to provisioning a service, including all fulfilment elements, both tangible and intangible. Input comes from financial systems, and consists of payment for actual resources consumed by IT in the provisioning of a service. These cost elements include items such as:

- hardware and software licences;
- annual maintenance fees for hardware and software;
- personnel resources used in the support or maintenance of a service;
- utilities, data centre or other facilities charges;
- taxes, capital or interest charges;
- compliance.

The sum of these actual service costs typically represents the baseline from which the minimum value of a service is calculated since providers are seldom willing to offer a service where they are unable to recover the provisioning cost.

Service value potential is the value-added component based on the customer's perception of value from the service or expected marginal Utility and Warranty from using the service, in comparison with what is possible using the customer's own assets (see Figure 5.20).

Figure 5.20 Customer assets are the basis for defining value 2 (Source: OGC ITIL Service Strategy ISBN 978-0-113310-45-6)

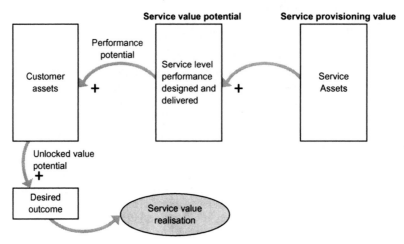

Provisioning value elements add up first to establish a baseline. The value-added components of the service are then monetised individually according to their perceived value to estimate the true value of the Service Package. All of these components are then summed along with the baseline costs to determine the ultimate value of the service. The interrelated concepts of provisioning value and perceived service value potential are shown in Figure 5.20.

Planning confidence
One goal of Financial Management is to ensure proper funding for the delivery and consumption of services. Planning provides financial translation and qualification of expected future demand for IT services. Financial Management planning departs from historical IT planning by focusing on demand and supply variances resulting from business strategy, capacity inputs and forecasting, rather than traditional individual line item expenditures or business cost accounts. As with planning for any other business organisation, input should be collected from all areas of the IT organisation and the business. Planning can be categorised into three main areas, each representing financial results that are required for continued visibility and service valuation:

- operating and capital (general and fixed asset ledgers);
- demand (need and use of IT services);
- regulatory and environmental (compliance).

Confidence is the notion that financial inputs and models for service demand and supply represent statistically significant measures of accuracy. Data confidence is important for two reasons:

- The critical role data plays in achieving the objectives of Financial Management.
- The possibility of erroneous data undermining decision-making.

Service investment analysis

Financial Management provides the shared analytical models and knowledge used throughout an enterprise in order to assess the expected value and/or return of a given initiative, solution, programme or project in a standardised fashion. It sets the thresholds that guide the organisation in determining what level of analytical sophistication is to be applied to various projects based on size, scope, resources, cost and related parameters.

The objective of service investment analysis is to derive a value indication for the total Lifecycle of a service based on:

- the value received;
- costs incurred during the Lifecycle.

Methods, models, activities and techniques

Financial Management uses many methods, models and techniques.

Service valuation   (value to IT) or cost to IT to provision service.

Decisions will need to be taken during the activities of service valuation.

- Direct versus indirect costs are those that are either:
  - direct costs that are clearly directly attributable to a specific service; versus
  - indirect costs that are shared among multiple services.

These costs should be approached logically to first determine which line items are sensible to maintain, given the data available and the level of effort required.

- Labour costs are another key item of expenditure requiring a decision. This decision is similar to that of 'direct versus indirect' above, compounded by the complexity and accuracy of time tracking systems. If the capability to account for resources allocated across services is not available, then rules and assumptions must be created for allocation of these costs.

- Variable cost elements include expenditures that are not fixed, but which vary depending on drivers such as the number of users or the number of running instances. Decisions need to be made based on the ability to pinpoint services or service components that cause increases in variability, since this variability can be a major source of price sensitivity.

- Translation from cost account data to service value is only possible once costs are attributed to services rather than, or in addition to, traditional cost accounts.

NB — 70 & 71

Service provisioning models and analysis

As companies analyse their current methods for providing services there are some basic alternatives to be considered that assist in framing the discussion and the analysis.

- **Managed services:** this model is the more traditional variant commonly found in the industry. In its simplest form, it is where a Business Unit requiring a service funds the provision of that service for itself. The service provider attempts to calculate the cost of the service in terms of development, infrastructure, manpower etc. so that the business and the service provider can plan for funding accordingly. In this simple example, the service is managed through the customer-specific application of service-related hardware, software and manpower, and the Business Unit pays for the entire service.

- **Shared services:** this model targets the provisioning of multiple services to one or more Business Units through use of shared infrastructure and resources. This concept is also widely applied throughout industry and represents significant cost savings to practitioners over the managed services model through the increased utilisation of existing resources.

- **Utility-based provisioning:** this model maximises the combination of services being provisioned over the same infrastructure so that even more services are provisioned utilising the same Resources found in the shared services model. This is accomplished by providing services on a utility basis, dependent on how much, how often and at what times the customer needs them. (Note that the word 'utility' is used here with a very specific meaning that is different from the meaning used in the rest of this book.) Examples of such services would include an accounting application with primary usage at the end of each month or a reporting service that receives heavy usage only around the 1st and 15th of each month.

- **Onshore, offshore or near-shore:** the advent of offshore service provisioning and its related success is not new. However, companies are still finding that what represents an offshore opportunity for one firm may not necessarily be an opportunity for another. Many service elements discussed in this book (and others discussed in the Service Design, Service Transition and Service Operation publications) are combined in an analysis of what mix of onshore, near-shore and offshore service provisioning is right for a specific company at a specific time.

The Financial Management impact on this decision cannot be underestimated. If a company does not understand its core service cost components and variable cost dynamics, it will typically have a difficult time making logical and fact-based decisions regarding outsourcing models, and an equally difficult time asking the right questions of providers.

- **Service provisioning cost analysis:** this is the activity of statistically evaluating and ranking the various forms of provisioning (and often providers) to determine the most beneficial and cost-effective model.

Funding model alternatives

Funding addresses the financial impacts from changes to current and future demand for IT services and the way in which IT will retain the funds to continue operations. This section offers a high-level discussion of various traditional models for the funding of IT services. Since each model assumes a different perspective, yet rests on the same financial data, an increased ability to generate the requisite information translates to increased visibility into service costs and perceived value. The model chosen should always take into account and be appropriate for the current business culture and expectations.

- **Rolling plan funding:** in a rolling plan, as one cycle completes another cycle of funding is added. This plan encourages a constant cycle of funding. However, it only addresses timing and does not necessarily increase accuracy. This type of model for funding works well with a Service Lifecycle treatment where a commitment to fund a service is made at the beginning of the Lifecycle and rolls until changes are made or the Lifecycle has ended.

- **Trigger-based plan:** this arises when identified critical triggers occur and set off plans for a particular event. For example, the Change Management Process would be a trigger to the Planning Process for all approved changes that have financial impacts. Another trigger might be Capacity Planning where insight into capacity variances would affect the financial translation of IT services. This type of planning alleviates timing issues when accounting for past events since the Process requires future planning at the time of the change. It would be a good plan to use with Portfolio Service Management since it deals with services on a Lifecycle basis.

- **Zero-based funding:** this refers to how funding of IT occurs. Funding is only enough to bring the balance of the IT financial centre back to zero or to bring the balance of the funding of a service back to zero until another funding cycle. This equates to funding only the actual costs to deliver the IT services.

Business Impact Analysis

A Business Impact Analysis (BIA) seeks to identify a company's most critical business services through analysis of outage severity translated into a financial value, coupled with operational risk. This information can help shape and enhance operational performance by enabling better decision-making regarding prioritisation of Incident handling, Problem Management focus, change and release management operations, project priority etc. It is a beneficial tool for identifying the cost of service outage to a company, and the relative worth of a service. These two concepts are not identical.

The cost of service outage is a financial value placed on a specific service, and is meant to reflect the value of lost productivity and revenue over a specific period of time. The value of a service relative to other services in a portfolio may not result exclusively from financial characteristics. Service value, as discussed earlier, is derived from characteristics that may go beyond Financial Management, and represent aspects such as the ability to complete work or communicate with clients that may not be directly related to revenue generation. Both of these elements can be identified to a very adequate degree by the use of a BIA.

ROLES, RESPONSIBILITIES AND FUNCTIONS

The main roles, responsibilities and functions associated with Service Strategy
are discussed in this section.

Roles and responsibilities
Product Manager

This role is similar to that of the Service Owner described previously. Product
Manager is a key role within the Service Strategy activities and Processes,
especially SPM. The role is responsible for managing services as a product over
the entire Service Lifecycle. Product Managers are recognised as the subject
matter experts on the services and LoSs for which they are responsible. They
understand service models and their internal structure and dynamics.

The main responsibilities of a Product Manager should include:

- accountability for a specified service or LoS through the entire Service Lifecycle;
- representing the service across the organisation;
- understanding the dynamics and structure of services, the service model,
  service components etc.;
- evaluating new market opportunities, operating models, technologies and the
  emerging needs of customers;
- providing leadership on the development of business cases, LoS strategy,
  financial analysis, new service deployment and Service Lifecycle management
  schedules;
- working with the CSI Manager to identify and prioritise service
  improvement;
- participating in external service review meetings (with the business);
- negotiating internal agreements with Business Relationship Managers
  (BRMs);
- providing a point of escalation (notification) for major incidents impacting the
  service.

Relationship Manager/Business Relationship Manager

Business Relationship Managers (BRMs) are responsible for gaining an
understanding of their customer's business and having a good knowledge of
customer and business outcomes. This is essential to developing strong business

relationships with customers. The role is often combined with the Service Level Manager role.

The main responsibilities of a BRM should include:

- developing strong relationships with their customers;
- managing customer needs and opportunities through the use of a Customer Portfolio (a database used to store details of all of the service provider's customers);
- representing customers working closely with Product Managers to ensure that the Service Catalogue has the right mix of LoS and SLPs to fulfil the needs of the Customer Portfolio;
- working closely with the Product Managers/Service Owners to ensure that services meet the business needs of their customers;
- developing internal and external markets where appropriate;
- providing an outcome-based definition of all customer requirements;
- identifying PBA and all sources of customer and business demand;
- identifying the most suitable combination of LoSs and SLPs for every customer outcome they are concerned with, relating customer outcomes to supporting UPs.

Service Portfolio Manager

The Service Portfolio Manager is responsible for the effectiveness of the SPM process. The main responsibilities of a Service Portfolio Manager should include:

- ensuring that the SPM process is effective and enforced;
- managing the Service Portfolio and its contents;
- ensuring that there is the right mix of services in the Service Pipeline and the Service Catalogue;
- ensuring that the information contained within the Service Catalogue is appropriate and adequate for informed decision-making;
- assisting BRMs and Financial Management with the governance of investments in services and Service Management.
- assisting with the definition, analysis, approval and chartering of services within the Service Portfolio.

Financial Manager

Financial Managers tailor a portfolio of investments based on their customer's risk and reward profile. Regardless of the profile, the objective is the same: maximise return at an acceptable risk level. When conditions change, appropriate changes are made to the portfolio. There is a need for applying comparable practices when managing a portfolio of services.

The main responsibilities of a Financial Manager should include:

- providing the business and IT with the quantification in financial terms of the value of IT services;
- assisting and approving Business Cases and investments in new or changed services;
- evaluating and quantifying Service Portfolio investment opportunities;
- ensuring the financial viability of the service provider organisation;
- understanding and providing information and assistance on service costing and pricing structures;
- financial calculation and reporting, including Return on Investment (ROI) and Value of Investment (VOI).

SYLLABUS REFERENCE: ITILMD07-1

Understand the role and responsibilities of the Service Owner.

Functions
Business Units and Service Units

BUSINESS UNIT

A segment of the business which has its own plans, metrics, income and costs. Each Business Unit owns assets and uses these to create value for customers in the form of goods and services.

A Business Unit is simply a bundle of assets intended to create value for customers in the form of goods and services, as shown in Figure 5.1. Customers pay for the value they receive which ensures that the Business Unit maintains an adequate return on assets. The relationship is good as long as the customer receives value and the Business Unit recovers costs and some form of additional compensation or profit. The relationship becomes strong when there is a balance between value created and returns generated.

Service Units are like Business Units: a bundle of service assets specialising in creating value in the form of services, as shown in Figures 5.2 and 5.20. In many cases Business Units (customers) and Service Units are part of the same organisation.

SYLLABUS REFERENCE: ITILMD07-3

Understand the operational issues surrounding Business Units and Service Units.

6 SERVICE DESIGN

LEARNING OBJECTIVES

The purpose of this chapter is to help candidates understand all aspects of the Service Design stage of the Lifecycle, including:

- the purpose, goals and objectives;
- the key concepts, definitions, principles and models;
- the Processes;
- the roles, responsibilities and functions.

 PURPOSE, GOALS AND OBJECTIVES   N.B.

The main purpose of Service Design is the design of new or changed services for transition to the live environment. It is important that a holistic approach to all aspects of design is adopted, and that when changing or amending any of the individual elements of design all other aspects are considered. This should include the impact on the overall service, the management systems, the tools, the architectures, the technology, the Processes and the necessary measurements and metrics.

> **KEY MESSAGE**
>
> A holistic approach should be adopted for all Service Design aspects and areas to ensure consistency and integration within all activities and Processes across the entire IT technology providing end-to-end business-related functionality and quality.

 The main goals and objectives of Service Design are:

- to design services to satisfy business objectives, based on the quality, compliance, risk and security requirements, delivering more effective and efficient IT and business solutions and services;
- to design services that can be easily and efficiently developed and enhanced;

- to design efficient and effective Processes for the design, transition, operation and improvement of high-quality IT services and supporting systems, especially the Service Portfolio;
- to identify and manage risks so that they can be removed or mitigated before services go live;
- to design secure and resilient IT infrastructures, environments, applications and data/information, resources and capability;
- to design measurement methods and metrics for assessing the effectiveness and efficiency of the design processes and their deliverables;
- to produce and maintain IT plans, Processes, policies, architectures and frameworks for the design of quality IT solutions;
- to assist in the development of policies and standards for the design and planning of IT services;
- to develop IT skills and capability by moving strategy and design activities into operational tasks;
- to contribute to the improvement of the quality of IT service within the imposed design constraints, especially by reducing the need for rework.

SYLLABUS REFERENCE: ITILMD02-4

Account for the main goals and objectives of Service Design.

Good Service Design practices deliver high-quality, cost-effective services, ensuring business requirements are met. Value is delivered to the business through:

- reduced Total Cost of Ownership (TCO);
- improved quality of service;
- improved consistency of service;
- easier implementation of new or changed services;
- improved service alignment;
- more effective service performance;
- improved IT governance;
- more effective Processes;
- improved information and decision-making.

SYLLABUS REFERENCE: ITILMD02-5

Fully comprehend and communicate what value Service Design provides to the business.

KEY CONCEPTS, DEFINITIONS, PRINCIPLES AND MODELS

The key principles described within this section are:

- people, Processes, products and partners (The Four Ps of Service Design);
- the five major aspects of Service Design;
- sourcing approaches and options.

People, Processes, products and partners

The design and management of IT services require the effective deployment of the Capabilities and Resources of the organisation. This principally consists of the four Ps: people, Processes, products/technology (including the services and the tools) and partners/suppliers (including vendors and manufacturers), as shown in Figure 6.1.

 Figure 6.1 The four Ps of Service Design (Source: OGC ITIL Service Design ISBN 978-0-113310-47-0)

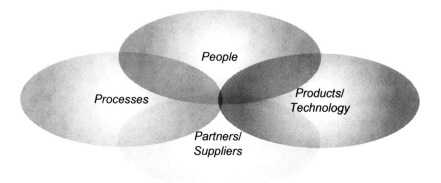

The implementation of Service Management as a practice is about preparing, planning and using the four Ps efficiently to ensure the effective deployment of new or changed services to meet the evolving needs of the business (Figure 6.2).

SYLLABUS REFERENCE: ITILMD04-8

Understand the importance of people, Processes, products and partners for Service Management.

The five major aspects of Service Design

An overall, integrated approach should be used for the design activities, including the five major aspects of Service Design:

Figure 6.2 Using the four Ps of Service Design

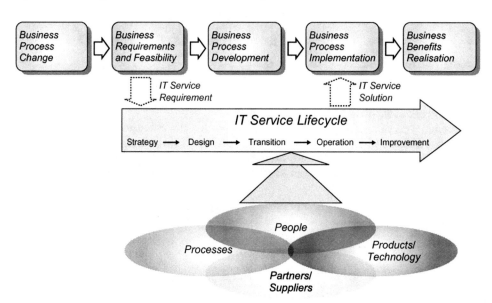

- service solution;
- Service Management systems and tools;
- technology architectures and management;
- Processes;
- measurement systems, methods and metrics.

Design of service solutions
The design of new or changed service solutions should include the following activities:

- Analysing the agreed business requirements.
- Reviewing the existing IT services and infrastructure and producing alternative service solutions, with a view to re-using or exploiting existing components and services wherever possible.
- Designing the service solutions to the new requirements, including their constituent components.
- Ensuring that the contents of the Service Acceptance Criteria (SAC) are incorporated and the required achievements are planned into the initial design.
- Evaluating and costing alternative designs.
- Agreeing the expenditure and budgets.

- Re-evaluating and confirming the business benefits, including the Return on Investment (ROI) from the service, including all service costs, business benefits and increased revenues.

- Agreeing the preferred solution and its planned outcomes and targets (Service Level Requirement (SLR)).

- Checking the solution is in balance with all corporate and IT strategies, policies, plans and architectural documents.

- Ensuring that all of the appropriate corporate and IT governance and security controls are included with the solution.

- Completing an IT 'organisational readiness assessment' to ensure that the service can be effectively operated to meet its agreed targets and that the organisation has the appropriate capability to deliver to the agreed level.

- Supplying and supporting the agreements necessary to maintain and deliver the service.

- Assembling a Service Design Package (SDP) containing everything necessary for the subsequent transition, operation and improvement of the new service solution.

Design of supporting management systems and tools

The most effective way of managing all areas of services and components through their Lifecycles is through the use of appropriate management systems and tools to support the automation of effective processes. The Service Portfolio is the most critical management tool for the effective support and integration of all processes, together with the Service Knowledge Management System (SKMS). The Service Portfolio should form an integral element of the SKMS and should contain all of the information necessary to manage services and investments, including service name, description, status, classification, criticality, business owners, IT owners, SLA, supporting OLAs, supporting contracts, costs, charges, revenue and metrics.

The Service Portfolio should contain the Service Pipeline, the Service Catalogue and Retired Services with information on every service and its current status.

The same approach should also be used for the design of all other Service Management systems and tools, including:

- Service Knowledge Management System (SKMS);

- Configuration Management System (CMS);

- Service Desk System;

- Capacity Management Information System (CMIS);

- Availability Management Information System (AMIS);

- Security Management Information System (SMIS);

- Supplier and Contract Database (SCD).

Design of technology architecture and management
The architectural design activities within an IT organisation are concerned with producing overall strategic 'blueprints' for the development and deployment of an IT infrastructure that will satisfy the current and future needs of the business.

ARCHITECTURE

The fundamental organisation of a system, embodied in its components, their relationships to each other and to the environment and the principles guiding its design and evolution.

SYSTEM

A collection of components organised to accomplish a specific function or set of functions.

In essence, architectural design is the development and maintenance of IT policies, strategies, architectures, designs, documents, plans and processes for the deployment and subsequent operation and improvement of appropriate IT services and solutions throughout an organisation.

ENTERPRISE ARCHITECTURE

Enterprise Architecture, as defined by Gartner, is the process of translating business vision and strategy into effective enterprise change, by creating, communicating and improving key principles and models that describe the enterprise's future states and enable its evolution.

The Enterprise Architecture should be an integrated element of the Business Architecture and should include all of the areas illustrated, together with their interfaces, relationships and dependencies, as shown in Figure 6.3.

KEY MESSAGE

The real benefit and ROI of the Enterprise Architecture comes not from the architecture itself, but from the ability of the organisation to design and implement projects and solutions in a rapid and consistent manner.

Figure 6.3 Enterprise Architecture (Source: OGC ITIL Service Design ISBN 978-0-113310-47-0)

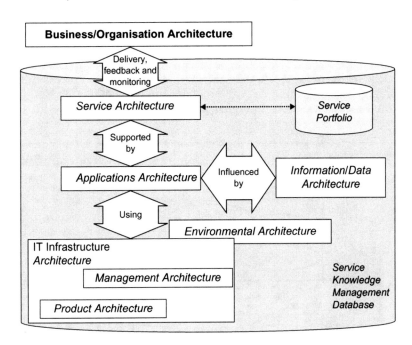

Design of Processes

All Processes should directly or indirectly create value for a customer or stakeholder.

PROCESS

A structured set of activities designed to accomplish a specific objective.

Processes have the following characteristics:

- They are measurable: all Processes should be measurable in terms of cost, quality or performance.

- They have deliverables: every Process exists to deliver specific results or outcomes.

- They have customers: every Process delivers primary results or a desired outcome to customers or stakeholders.

- They respond to triggers: while Processes may be ongoing or iterative, they should be traceable to a specific event or trigger.

A Process takes one or more defined inputs and turns them into defined outputs. A Process may include any of the roles, responsibilities, tools and management controls required to reliably deliver the outputs. A Process may define policies, standards, guidelines, activities and work instructions if they are needed. Processes, once designed and defined, should be documented and controlled. Once under control they can be repeated and become manageable. Processes that use feedback for self-corrective action or improvement are examples of closed-loop systems. The degree of feedback and control required over the Process can be defined and process measurements and metrics can be used to control and improve the Process, as shown in Figure 6.4.

Figure 6.4 Generic process elements (Source: OGC ITIL Service Design ISBN 978-0-113310-47-0)

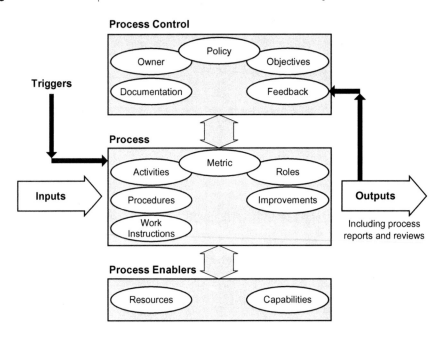

Each organisation should adopt a formalised approach to the design and implementation of Processes. The same approach should be used within an organisation for all Processes. The objective should be not to design 'perfect Processes', but to design practical and appropriate Processes with 'in-built' improvement mechanisms, so that the effectiveness and efficiency of Processes can be continually improved.

Design of measurement and metrics

KEY MESSAGE

'If you can't measure it, then you can't manage it.'

In order to manage and control services, systems, components and Processes, they need to be monitored and measured. The fifth aspect of Service Design is the design of the measurements systems and metrics. Metrics and measurements should be carefully selected, because metrics influence and change the behaviour of the people working within the supporting activities. Therefore only measurements and metrics that encourage progression towards achieving business objectives and desired behaviour should be selected.

The measurements and metrics selected need to be appropriate for the capability and maturity of the organisation, the people, the Processes and the systems. There are four types of metric that can be used to measure capability and performance:

- **Progress:** milestones and deliverables in the capability of the Process.

- **Compliance:** compliance of the Process to governance requirements, regulatory requirements and compliance of people to the use of the Process.

- **Effectiveness:** the accuracy and correctness of the Process and its ability to deliver the 'right result'.

- **Efficiency:** the productivity of the Process, its speed, throughput and resource utilisation.

The selection of metrics should be carefully designed and planned and should include:

- the metrics;

- the point of measurement;

- the method and frequency of measurement;

- the method and frequency of calculation;

- the method and frequency of reporting.

The primary metrics should always focus on determining the effectiveness and the quality of the solutions provided. Secondary metrics can then measure the efficiency of the service, systems, components and Processes used to produce and manage the solution. The priority should always be to ensure that the solutions provide the correct outcomes for the business. Therefore the measurement methods and metrics should always provide this business-focused measurement.

The most effective method of measurement is to establish a 'Metrics Tree' or 'KPI tree'. Many organisations collect measurements in individual areas, but fail to aggregate them and gain the full benefit of the measurements.

Organisations should attempt to develop a 'Metrics Tree', such as the one shown in Figure 6.5, based on a Balanced Scorecard (i.e. based on customer, business, innovative and financial perspective metrics), supported by integrated, automated measurement systems.

Figure 6.5 The Metrics Tree (Source: OGC ITIL Service Design ISBN 978-0-113310-47-0)

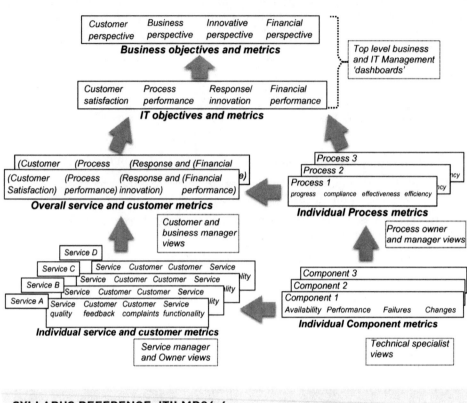

SYLLABUS REFERENCE: ITILMD04-6

Understand and explain the five major aspects of Service Design.

Sourcing approaches and options

When designing new or changed service solutions, one of the key decisions to be made is the type of model to be used for the design, transition, operation and improvement of the service. The model selected will depend on the Resources and Capability that exist within the current organisation. A review should therefore be conducted to determine the current Resources and Capabilities of the organisation and should include:

- the business drivers and requirements;
- the demands, targets and requirements of the new service;
- the scope and capability of external suppliers;
- the maturity of the organisations currently involved;
- the culture of the organisations involved;
- the IT infrastructure;

- the degree of corporate and IT governance and the level of ownership required;
- the budgets and resources required;
- the staff levels and skills.

The main strategies or models that can be used for the sourcing of services are shown in Table 6.1.

Table 6.1 Main service sourcing strategies (Source: OGC ITIL Service Design ISBN 978-0-113310-47-0)

Strategy/Model	Description
Insourcing	This approach relies on utilising internal organisational resources in the design, development, transition, maintenance, operation and/or support of new, changed or revised services or data centre operations.
Outsourcing	This approach utilises the resources of an external organisation or organisations in a formal arrangement to provide a well-defined portion of a service's design, development, maintenance, operations and/or support. This includes the consumption of services from Application Service Providers (ASPs, described below).
Co-sourcing	Often a combination of insourcing and outsourcing, using a number of outsourcing organisations working together to co-source key elements within the Lifecycle. This generally involves using a number of external organisations working together to design, develop, transition, maintain, operate and/or support a portion of the service.
Partnership or multi-sourcing	Formal arrangements between two or more organisations to work together to design, develop,

(Continued)

Table 6.1 *(Continued)*

Strategy/Model	Description
	transition, maintain, operate and/or support IT service(s). The focus here tends to be on strategic partnerships that leverage critical expertise or market opportunities.
Business Process Outsourcing (BPO)	The increasing trend of relocating entire business functions using formal arrangements between organisations where one organisation provides and manages the other organisation's entire business process(es) or function(s) in a low-cost location. Common examples are accounting, payroll and call-centre operations.
Application Service Provision	This involves formal arrangements with an Application Service Provider (ASP) organisation that will provide shared computer-based services to customer organisations over a network. Applications offered in this way are also sometimes referred to as on demand software/applications. Through ASPs, the complexities and costs of such shared software can be reduced and provided to organisations that could otherwise not justify the investment.
Knowledge Process Outsourcing (KPO)	The newest form of outsourcing, KPO, is a step ahead of BPO in that KPO organisations provide domain-based processes and business expertise rather than just process expertise, and it requires advanced analytical and specialised skills from the outsourcing organisation.

The advantages and disadvantages of these strategies/models can be summarised as shown in Table 6.2.

Table 6.2 Advantages and disadvantages of service sourcing strategies (Source: OGC ITIL Service Design ISBN 978-0-113310-47-0)

Strategy/Model	Advantages	Disadvantages
Insourcing	Direct control	Scale limitations
	Freedom of choice	Cost and time to market for
	Rapid prototyping of	services readily available
	leading-edge services	outside
	Familiar policies and	Dependent on internal
	processes	resources, skills and
	Company-specific knowledge	competencies
Outsourcing	Economies of scale	Less direct control
	Purchased expertise	Exit barriers
	Supports focus on company	Solvency risk of suppliers
	core competencies	Unknown supplier skills
	Support of transient needs	and competencies
	Test drive/trial of new services	More challenging business
		process integration
		Increased governance and
		verification
Co-sourcing	Time to market	Project complexity
	Leveraged expertise	Intellectual property and
	Control	copyright protection
	Use of specialised providers	Culture clash between
		companies
Partnership or multi-sourcing	Time to market	Project complexity
	Market expansion/entrance	Intellectual property and

(Continued)

Table 6.2 *(Continued)*

Strategy/Model	Advantages	Disadvantages
	Competitive response	copyright protection
	Leveraged expertise	Culture clash between
	Trust, alignment and	companies
	mutual benefit	
	'Risk and reward'	
	agreements	
Business Process Outsourcing (BPO)	Single point of responsibility	Culture clash between
	'One-stop shop'	companies
	Access to specialist skills	Loss of business
	Risks transferred to the	knowledge
	outsourcer	Loss of relationship with
	Low-cost location	the business
Application Service Provision	Access to expensive and	Culture clash between
	complex solutions	companies
	Low-cost location	Access to facilities only, not
	Support and upgrades	knowledge
	included	Often usage-based charging
	Security and IT Service	
	Continuity Management	
	(ITSCM) options included	
Knowledge Process Outsourcing (KPO)	Access to specialist skills,	Culture clash between
	knowledge and expertise	companies
	Low-cost location	Loss of internal expertise
	Significant cost savings	Loss of relationship with the
		business

PROCESSES

The main Processes within the Service Design stage of the Service Lifecycle are:

- Service Catalogue Management (SCM); — NEW Group
- Service Level Management (SLM)*;
- Capacity Management*;
- Availability Management*;
- IT Service Continuity Management (ITSCM)*;
- Information Security Management (ISM);
- Supplier Management.

The four Processes identified with an asterisk were contained in ITIL v2 and only the changes have been covered within this section. The only changes were to the ITSCM Process. The three 'new to ITIL' Processes are considered in more detail.

Service Catalogue Management
The purpose of Service Catalogue Management (SCM) is to provide a single source of consistent information on all of the agreed services and ensure that it is widely available to all of those approved for access to it.

The objectives of SCM are:

- to ensure that a Service Catalogue is produced, maintained and available to those approved to access it;
- to manage and protect the information contained within the Service Catalogue and ensure that it is consistent with other information within the Service Portfolio;
- to ensure that the information contained within the Service Catalogue is accurate and reflects the current status, interfaces and dependencies of all services.

The scope of the SCM Process is to provide and maintain accurate information on all services that are designed or transitioned to the live environment or already in the live environment.

The Service Catalogue provides a central source of information on services and ensures that all areas of the business can view an accurate and consistent view of services and their status. It should also contain details of the use of services and the quality and level of service that can be expected.

Each organisation should develop and maintain a policy with regard to both the Portfolio and the Catalogue, relating to the services recorded within them, what details are recorded and what statuses are recorded for each of the services. The policy should also contain details of responsibilities for each section of the overall Service Portfolio and the scope of each of the constituent sections.

Many organisations fail to agree a clear definition of what is a service in an IT context. IT staff often confuse a 'service', as perceived by the customer, with an IT system. In many cases one 'service' can be made up of other 'services' (and so on), which are themselves made up of one or more IT systems within an overall infrastructure including hardware, software, networks, together with environments, data and applications. A good starting point is often to ask customers which IT services they use and how those services map onto and support their business processes. Customers often have a greater clarity of what they believe a service to be. Each organisation needs to develop a policy of what is a service and how it is defined, and agree it within their own organisation. To avoid confusion it is often a good idea to define a hierarchy of Services within the Service Catalogue, by defining different categories of services such as a business service or a supporting service.

The Service Catalogue is a valuable source of information for all areas of IT, especially for completing activities such as Business Impact Analysis or Risk Analysis exercises. A Service Catalogue can contain two elements:

- The Business Service Catalogue: containing details of all the IT services delivered to the customer, together with relationships to the Business Units and the business process that rely on the IT services. This is the customer view of the Service Catalogue.

- The Technical Service Catalogue: containing details of all the IT services delivered to the customer, together with relationships to the supporting services, shared services, components and CIs necessary to support the provision of the service to the business. This should underpin the Business Service Catalogue and not form part of the customer view.

The relationship between these two elements is shown in Figure 6.6.

Some organisations maintain either a Business Service Catalogue or a Technical Service Catalogue. The more mature organisations maintain both elements within a single Service Catalogue, which itself is part of a Service Portfolio. The Business Service Catalogue allows a much more proactive business-driven approach to be adopted by the service provider in its relationship with its customers.

The main activities within the Service Catalogue Management process are:

- agreeing and documenting a service definition with all relevant parties;
- liaising with Service Portfolio Management to agree the contents of the Service Portfolio and the Service Catalogue;
- producing and maintaining a Service Catalogue and its contents, in conjunction with the Service Portfolio;

Figure 6.6 The Business Service Catalogue and the Technical Service Catalogue
(Source: OGC ITIL Service Design ISBN 978-0-113310-47-0)

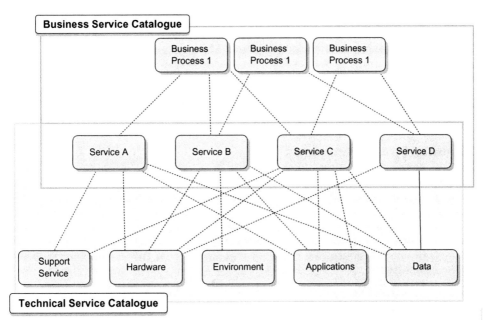

- liaising with the business and IT Service Continuity Management on the dependencies of Business Units and their business processes with the supporting IT services, contained within the Business Service Catalogue;

- liaising with support teams, suppliers and Configuration Management on interfaces and dependencies between IT services and supporting services and components.

SYLLABUS REFERENCE: ITILMD12-1

Define and explain the Service Catalogue, Business Service Catalogue and the Technical Service Catalogue.

Some of the main KPIs of the Service Catalogue Management process that should be considered for measuring the effectiveness of the process are:

- the percentage of services recorded within the Service Catalogue;

- the number of variances detected between the Service Catalogue and the 'real-world' situation.

Other measurements and KPIs that could be used are:

- business users' awareness of the services being provided;
- IT staff awareness of the technology supporting the services.

The challenges facing the Service Catalogue Management process are:

- maintaining an accurate Service Catalogue as part of a Service Portfolio;
- gaining appropriate involvement and buy-in of key business personnel;
- service provider staff involvement and buy-in.

Information Security Management

The goal or purpose of Information Security Management (ISM) is to align IT security with business security and ensure that information security is effectively managed in all services and Service Management activities. The objectives of ISM are:

- to ensure that information is available and usable when required, and that systems can appropriately resist attacks and recover from or prevent failures (availability);
- to ensure that information is observed by or disclosed to only those who have a right to know (confidentiality);
- to ensure that information is complete, accurate and protected against unauthorised modification (integrity);
- to ensure that business transactions, as well as information exchanges between enterprises, or with partners, can be trusted (authenticity and non-repudiation).

ISM should provide a focal point for all IT security issues. The scope should include all IT systems and services. ISM must ensure that an Information Security Policy that covers the use and misuse of all IT systems and services is produced, maintained and enforced. ISM needs to understand the total IT and business security environment, including:

- the Business Security Policy and plans;
- the current business operation and its security requirements;
- the future business plans and requirements;
- legislative requirements;
- obligations and responsibilities with regard to security contained within SLAs;
- the business and IT risks, and their management.

ISM ensures that an Information Security Policy is maintained and enforced that fulfils the needs of the Business Security Policy and the requirements of corporate governance. ISM raises awareness of the need for security within all services and assets throughout the organisation, ensuring that the policy is appropriate for the needs of the organisation. ISM manages all aspects of IT and information security within all areas of IT and Service Management activity. ISM also provides assurance of business processes by enforcing appropriate security controls in all areas of IT and by managing IT risk in line with business and corporate risk management processes and guidelines.

ISM must be closely aligned to business security processes and needs. Boards and executive management are responsible for ensuring information security is an integral part of corporate governance. A comprehensive ISM process and security framework should include:

- an Information Security Policy and specific security policies that address each aspect of strategy, controls and regulation;
- an Information Security Management System (ISMS), containing the standards, management procedures and guidelines supporting the Information Security Policies;
- a comprehensive security strategy, closely linked to the business objectives, strategies and plans;
- an effective security organisational structure;
- a set of security controls to support the policy;
- the management of security risks;
- monitoring Processes to ensure compliance and provide feedback on effectiveness;
- a communications strategy and plan for security;
- a training and awareness strategy and plan.

ISM activities should be driven by an Information Security Policy, which should be appropriate to the needs of the business and cover all areas of security, including:

- an overall Information Security Policy;
- a use and misuse of IT assets policy;
- an access control policy;
- a password control policy;
- an email policy;
- an internet policy;
- an anti-virus policy;
- an information classification policy;
- a document classification policy;
- a remote access policy;
- a policy with regard to supplier access of IT service, information and components;
- an asset disposal policy.

The Information Security Management System (ISMS) provides a structure for coordinating ISM activities and a basis for a cost-effective security programme (see Figure 6.7).

Figure 6.7 Framework for managing IT security (Source: OGC ITIL Service Design ISBN 978-0-113310-47-0)

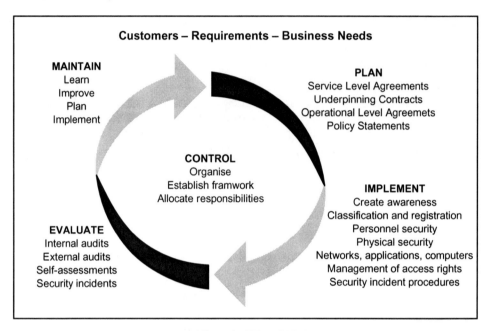

The five elements of the ISMS framework shown in the figure are:

- **Control:** establishes a management framework, establishes an organisational structure, allocates responsibilities and establishes and controls documentation.

- **Plan:** devises and recommends appropriate policies and security measures, from business and service risk, plans, strategies and agreements and legal, ethical and moral responsibilities.

- **Implement:** ensures that appropriate procedures, tools and controls are in place to underpin the Information Security Policy.

- **Evaluate:** supervises and checks compliance with the security policy and security requirements, carries out regular audits of the technical security and provides information to external auditors and regulators.

- **Maintain:** improves security agreements and improves the implementation of security measures and controls.

This should all be achieved using a formal PDCA (Plan → Do → Check → Act) cycle of continual improvement.

Information security governance is also a key element of an ISM process. Information security governance, when properly implemented, should provide six basic outcomes:

- **Strategic alignment:** ensures that security requirements and practices are driven and aligned with enterprise requirements and practices.

- **Value delivery:** ensures a set of security best practices are properly prioritised and used based on greatest business impact and benefit, with a culture of continual improvement.

- **Risk management:** ensures that risk profiles, exposure, management priorities, mitigation and acceptance are well understood and applied.

- **Performance management:** ensures that agreed meaningful metrics and measurement processes are used to identify and improve weaknesses and are independently assured.

- **Resource management:** security architectures, documentation and knowledge are captured, made available and utilised.

- **Business process assurance:** ensures the availability of business processes.

Information security must be an integral of all systems and services and is an ongoing process that needs to be continuously managed using a set of security controls as shown in Figure 6.8.

Figure 6.8 Security controls for threats and incidents (Source: OGC ITIL Service Design ISBN 978-0-113310-47-0)

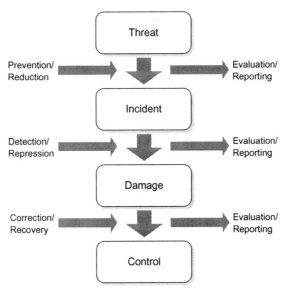

The set of security controls should be designed to support and enforce the Information Security Policy and to minimise all recognised and identified threats.

The following stages can be identified with regards to a security issue.
Initially there is a risk that a threat will actually materialise. When the threat
materialises a security incident is recorded. The incident may result in damage
that has to be repaired. Appropriate measures and controls can be selected and
implemented at each of these stages:

- **Preventative:** used to prevent incidents from occurring, for example the
  allocation or access rights to a limited group of authorised people.

- **Reductive:** used to minimise the impact and damage that may occur, for
  example taking regular backups.

- **Detective:** used to detect incidents as soon as possible, for example virus
  checking software.

- **Repressive:** used to counteract or prevent another occurrence, for example
  the blocking of an account or network address.

- **Corrective:** used to repair the damage, for example roll-back or restoration
  of backups.

An evaluation and review is necessary in all cases of security breaches and
incidents to determine what went wrong, what caused them and how they can be
prevented from occurring in the future. Analysis and trending should be used to
identify major areas and identify and implement improvement actions to reduce
the volume and impact of security incidents and breaches.

The key activities within the ISM process are:

- production, review and revision of an overall Information Security Policy and
  a set of supporting specific policies;

- communication, implementation and enforcement of the security policies;

- monitoring and management of all security breaches and major security
  incidents;

- assessment and classification of all information assets, risks, vulnerabilities
  and documentation;

- implementation, review, revision and improvement of a set of security
  controls and risk assessment and responses;

- analysis and reporting of security risks and threats;

- analysis, reporting and reduction of the volumes and impact of security
  breaches and incidents;

- scheduling and completion of security reviews, audits and penetration
  tests.

The interactions, relationships and deliverables from these activities are shown
in Figure 6.9.

Figure 6.9 Information Security Management process activities (Source: OGC ITIL Service Design ISBN 978-0-113310-47-0)

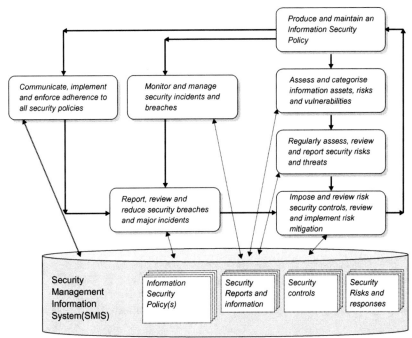

Some of the main KPIs of the Information Security Management process that should be considered for measuring the effectiveness of the process are:

- business protected against security violations:

  - Percentage decrease in security breaches reported to the Service Desk.

  - Percentage decrease in the impact of security breaches and incidents.

  - Percentage increase in SLA conformance to security clauses.

- the determination of a clear and agreed policy, integrated with the needs of the business:

  - Decrease in the number of non-conformances of the ISM process with the business security policy and process.

- security procedures that are justified, appropriate and supported by senior management:

  - Increase in the acceptance and conformance of security procedures.

  - Increased support and commitment of senior management.

- a mechanism for improvement:

  - The number of suggested improvements to security procedures and controls.

  - Decrease in the number of security non-conformances detected during audits and security testing.

- information security is an integral part of all IT services and all ITSM processes:

  - Increase in the number of services and Processes conformant with security procedures and controls.

- effective marketing and education in security requirements, IT staff awareness of the technology supporting the services:

  - Increased awareness of the security policy and its contents, throughout the organisation.

  - Percentage increase in completeness of the technical Service Catalogue against IT components supporting the services.

  - Service Desk supporting all services.

The challenges facing the Information Security Management process are:

- gaining appropriate involvement, support and buy-in of key business personnel and management;

- maintaining alignment between the Business Security Policy and Processes and the Information Security Policy and Processes;

- changing a perception within the business that Information Security is a service provider responsibility, not a business issue;

- developing a security culture throughout the organisation.

Supplier Management + CONTRACTS MGT.

The purpose of the Supplier Management process is to manage suppliers and the services they supply, to provide seamless quality of service to the business ensuring value for money is obtained. The main objectives of the Supplier Management process are:

- to obtain value for money from supplier and contracts;

- to ensure that underpinning contracts and agreements with suppliers are aligned to business needs, and support and align with agreed targets in SLRs and SLAs, in conjunction with SLM;

- to manage relationships with suppliers;

- to manage supplier performance;

- to negotiate and agree contracts with suppliers and manage them through their Lifecycle;

- to maintain a supplier policy and a supporting Supplier and Contract Database (SCD).

All suppliers and contracts needed to support the provision of IT services to the business should be included within the scope of the Supplier Management process. However, the Process should be adapted to allow for the importance of the supplier and/or contract and the potential business impact on the provision of services.

The Supplier Management process should include:

- implementation and enforcement of the supplier policy;

- maintenance of a Supplier and Contract Database (SCD);

- supplier and contract categorisation and risk assessment;

- supplier and contract evaluation and selection;

- development, negotiation and agreement of contracts;

- contract review, renewal and termination;

- management of suppliers and supplier performance;

- agreement and implementation of service and supplier improvement plans;

- maintenance of standard contracts, terms and conditions;

- management of contractual dispute resolution;

- management of subcontracted suppliers.

A good Supplier Management process ensures that suppliers meet the terms, conditions and targets of their contracts and agreements, while trying to increase the value for money from supplier services. All Supplier Management activities should be driven by a supplier strategy and policy agreed with Service Strategy. A Supplier and Contract Database (SCD) should be established to ensure that consistency and effectiveness is achieved in the management of suppliers. The SCD should ideally be an integral element of a comprehensive Configuration Management System (CMS) and Service Knowledge Management System (SKMS) and should contain all of the information necessary to support the management of suppliers and contracts. The services provided by suppliers are also an essential element within the Service Catalogue. The relationships between the supporting services and the business services they support are key to delivering quality services to the business.

Each contract or service agreement with a supplier should contain:

- **basic terms and conditions:** duration, scope, definitions and commercial arrangements;

- **service description and scope:** the functionality, extent, delivery and performance;

- **service standards:** service measures and minimum levels of performance and quality;
- **workload ranges:** the volume ranges and the pricing policies;
- **management information:** the reports, measures and KPIs;
- **responsibilities and dependencies:** the roles, contacts, communication and escalation.

Not all suppliers should be managed in the same way, so some categorisation should be performed to ensure that the appropriate amount of time is spent managing suppliers and contracts. The best way of categorising suppliers is based on assessing the risk and impact associated with using the supplier (or losing them) and the value and importance of the supplier and their services to the business, as shown in Figure 6.10.

Figure 6.10 Supplier categorisation (Source: OGC ITIL Service Design ISBN 978-0-113310-47-0)

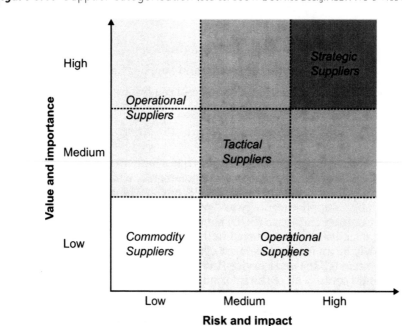

The amount of time and effort spent managing the supplier and the relationship can then be appropriate to its categorisation:

- **Strategic:** for significant 'partnering' relationships managed by senior management with regular and frequent contact, involving the exchange of strategic information and long-term plans (e.g. a network services provider).

- **Tactical:** for relationships involving significant commercial activity and business interaction, managed by middle management, involving regular contact and performance reviews (e.g. a hardware maintenance organisation).

- **Operational:** for suppliers of operational products or services, managed by junior operational management and would involve infrequent, but regular contact and performance reviews (e.g. a desktop support provider).

- **Commodity:** for suppliers that provide low-value and/or readily available products and services, which could be easily alternatively sourced (e.g. a paper supplier).

The effort and activity can then be focused on the relationships with key strategically important suppliers and less time and effort spent on the less important suppliers.

The key activities within the Supplier Management process are:

- supplier categorisation and maintenance of the SCD;
- evaluation and set up of new suppliers and contracts;
- establishing new suppliers;
- supplier and contract management and performance;
- contract renewal and termination.

The interactions, relationships and deliverables from these activities and the supplier strategy and policy are shown in Figure 6.11, together with the use of the SCD.

Some of the main KPIs of the Supplier Management process that should be considered for measuring the effectiveness of the process are:

- business protected from poor supplier performance or disruption:

    - Increase in the number of suppliers meeting the targets within the contract.

    - Reduction in the number of breaches of contractual targets.

- supporting services and their targets align with business needs and targets:

    - Increase in the number of service and contractual reviews held with suppliers.

    - Increase in the number of supplier and contractual targets aligned with SLA and SLR targets.

- availability of services is not compromised by supplier performance:

    - Reduction in the number of service breaches caused by suppliers.

    - Reduction in the number of threatened service breaches caused by suppliers.

Figure 6.11 Supplier Management process activities (Source: OGC ITIL Service Design ISBN 978-0-113310-47-0)

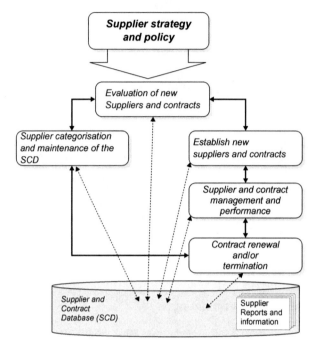

- clear ownership and awareness of supplier and contractual issues:

  - Increase in the number of suppliers with nominated supplier managers.
  - Increase in the number of contracts with nominated contract managers.

The challenges facing the Supplier Management process are:

- continually changing business and IT needs and managing significant change in parallel with delivering existing service;
- working with an imposed non-ideal contract that has poor targets or terms and conditions, or poor definition of service or supplier performance targets;
- legacy issues, especially with services recently outsourced;
- insufficient expertise retained within the organisation;
- being tied into long-term contracts, with no possibility of improvement, which have punitive penalty charges for early exit;
- situations where the supplier depends on the service provider in fulfilling the service delivery;
- disputes over charges;
- being caught in a daily fire-fighting mode, losing the proactive approach;

- communication issues – not interacting often enough or quick enough or focusing on the right issues;

- personality conflicts;

- one party using the contract to the detriment of the other party, resulting in win–lose changes rather than joint win–win changes;

- losing the strategic perspective, focusing on operational issues, causing a lack of focus on strategic relationship objectives and issues.

IT Service Continuity Management (ITSCM) changes   *Very little changes from v2*

The main enhancement introduced to the ITSCM process was the introduction of an additional recovery option in the list of available options:

- manual workarounds;

- reciprocal arrangements;

- gradual recovery (cold standby);

- intermediate recovery (warm standby);

- fast recovery (hot standby);

- immediate recovery (hot standby).

The additional option is that of fast recovery, which has been introduced between the intermediate and immediate recovery options and is explained below.

Fast recovery: this option (sometimes referred to as 'hot standby') provides for fast recovery and restoration of services and is sometimes provided as an extension to the intermediate recovery provided by a third-party recovery provider. Some organisations will provide their own facilities within the organisation, but not on an alternative site to the one used for the normal operations. Others implement their own internal second locations on an alternative site to provide more resilient recovery.

Where there is a need for a fast restoration of a service, it is possible to 'rent' floor space at the recovery site and install servers or systems with application systems and communications already available and data mirrored from the operational servers. In the event of a system failure, the customers can then recover and switch over to the back-up facility with little loss of service. This typically involves the re-establishment of the critical systems and services within a 24-hour period.

This has necessitated a change in the description of the immediate recovery option, which is now described as:

Immediate recovery: this option (also often referred to as 'hot standby', 'mirroring', 'load balancing' or 'split site') provides for immediate restoration of services, with no loss of service. For business critical services, organisations requiring continuous operation will provide their own facilities within the organisation, but not on the same site as the normal operations. Sufficient IT

103

equipment will be 'dual located' in either an owned or hosted location to run the compete service from either location in the event of loss of one facility, with no loss of service to the customer.

SYLLABUS REFERENCE: ITILMD13-2

Understand the changes made at ITIL v3 to IT Service Continuity Management.

ROLES, RESPONSIBILITIES AND FUNCTIONS

The main additional new roles, responsibilities and functions associated with Service Design are:

Roles and responsibilities
Service Design Manager
Service Design Manager is a key role within the Service Design processes and activities. It has overall responsibility for the coordination and deployment of quality solution designs for services and Processes. The main responsibilities of the role are:

- taking the Service Strategies and ensuring they are reflected in the Service Design practices and designs to meet documented business requirements;

- designing the functional aspects of the services as well as the infrastructure, environment applications and data management;

- producing quality, secure and resilient designs for new or improved services, technology architecture, Processes or measurement systems that meet agreed current and future IT requirements of the organisation;

- producing and maintaining all design documentation, including SDPs;

- measuring the effectiveness and efficiency of the Service Design processes and activities.

IT Planner
An IT Planner is responsible for the production and coordination of IT plans. The main responsibilities within the role are:

- developing IT plans that meet and continue to meet the IT requirements of the business, and coordinate and review their implementation;

- producing, maintaining and enforcing a set of IT standards policies, plans and strategies, required to support an organisation's business strategy;

- recommending policy for the effective use of IT throughout the organisation and working with IT designers to ensure that overall plans and strategies deliver their intended business outcomes;

- assuming full responsibility for the management, planning and coordination of IT systems and services;

- sponsoring and monitoring research, development and long-term planning for the provision and use of IT architectures, products and services;

- taking ultimate responsibility for prioritising and scheduling the implementation of new or changed services within IT;

- working with the business, senior management and other senior specialists and planners in formulating plans and making procurement decisions;

- investigating major options for providing IT services effectively and efficiently and recommend new innovative solutions;

- producing feasibility studies, business models, IT models, Business Cases, Statements of Requirement (SORs) and Invitations to Tender (ITTs) for recommended new IT systems and services;

- providing authoritative advice and guidance on relevant national and international standards, regulations, protocols and tariffs.

IT Designer/Architect

An IT Designer/Architect is responsible for the overall coordination and design of the required technology. Often Designers and Architects within a large organisation will specialise in a particular area of technology. In smaller organisations the roles are often combined. The main responsibilities of the role are:

- producing and reviewing the designs of all new or changed services, SLAs, OLAs and contracts;

- producing process maps of all of the Processes and their interfaces;

- designing secure and resilient technology architectures that meet all agreed requirements;

- ensuring that the design of all Processes, roles, responsibilities and documentation is regularly reviewed and audited for efficiency, effectiveness and compliance;

- designing an appropriate and suitable Service Portfolio, SKMS and set of management tools;

- designing measurement systems and techniques to support the continual improvement of services;

- producing and keeping up to date all IT design, architectural, policy and specification documentation;

- recommending proactive, innovative IT solutions for the improvement of IT design and operation;

- translating logical designs into physical designs to meet business needs;

- providing advice and guidance to all areas of IT and Business Management, analysts, planners and designers on all aspects of IT design.

Service Catalogue Manager

The Service Catalogue Manager is responsible for producing and maintaining the Service Catalogue. The main responsibilities of the role are:

- ensuring that all operational services and all services being prepared for operational running are recorded within the Service Catalogue;

- ensuring that all the information within the Service Catalogue is accurate and up to date;

- ensuring that all the information within the Service Catalogue is consistent with the information within the Service Portfolio and is adequately protected and backed up.

Security Manager

The Security Manager is responsible for ensuring that the aims of Security Management are met. The main responsibilities of the role are:

- developing and maintaining the Information Security Policy and a supporting set of specific policies, ensuring appropriate authorisation, commitment and endorsement from senior IT and business management;

- communicating and publicising the Information Security Policy to all appropriate parties, while promoting education and awareness of security;

- ensuring that the Information Security Policy is enforced and adhered to;

- identifying, classifying, controlling and protecting IT and information assets;

- assisting with Business Impact Analysis, Risk Analysis and risk management;

- designing, operating and maintaining a set of security controls and plans;

- monitoring and managing all security breaches and trends, handling security incidents, taking action to prevent recurrence wherever possible;

- ensuring all changes are assessed for impact on all security aspects, including the Information Security Policy and security controls, and attending Change Advisory Board (CAB) meetings when appropriate;

- performing security tests, reviews and audits;

- ensuring that all access to services by external partners and suppliers is subject to contractual agreements and responsibilities are defined;

- acting as a focal point for all security issues.

Supplier Manager

The Supplier Manager is responsible for ensuring that the aims of Supplier Management are met. The main responsibilities of the role are:

- ensuring that value for money is obtained from all suppliers and contracts;

- providing assistance in the development and review of SLAs, contracts, agreements or any other documents for third-party suppliers;

- ensuring that all IT supplier processes are consistent and interface to all corporate supplier strategies, processes and standard terms and conditions;

- maintaining and reviewing a Supplier and Contract Database (SCD);

- conducting regular review and risk analysis of all suppliers and contracts;

- ensuring that any underpinning contracts or agreements developed are aligned with those of the business;

- performing contract or SLA reviews at least annually;

- maintaining a process for dealing with contractual disputes, and ensuring that any disputes are dealt with in an effective manner;

- maintaining a process for dealing with the expected end, early end or transfer of a service;

- monitoring, reporting and regularly reviewing supplier performance against targets, identifying and implementing improvement actions;

- ensuring changes are assessed for their impact on suppliers, supporting services and contracts;

- coordinating and supporting all individual IT supplier and contract managers, ensuring that each supplier/contract has a nominated owner.

SYLLABUS REFERENCE: ITILMD05-3a

Explain the objectives, scope, concepts, activities, key metrics, roles and challenges for Service Catalogue Management, Information Security Management and Supplier Management.

7 SERVICE TRANSITION

LEARNING OBJECTIVES

The purpose of this chapter is to help candidates understand all the aspects of the Service Transition stage of the Lifecycle, including:

- the purpose, goals, objectives and value;
- the key concepts, definitions, principles and models;
- the Processes;
- the roles, responsibilities and functions.

PURPOSE, GOALS, OBJECTIVES AND VALUE

The purpose of Service Transition is to:

- plan and manage the capacity and resources required;
- package, build, test and deploy a release into production;
- provide a consistent and rigorous framework for evaluating the service capability and risk profile before a new or changed service is released or deployed;
- establish and maintain the integrity of all identified service assets and configurations;
- provide good-quality knowledge and information so that Change, Release and Deployment Management can expedite effective decisions;
- provide efficient repeatable build and installation mechanisms that can be used to deploy releases to the test and production environments;
- ensure that the service can be managed, operated and supported in accordance with the requirements and constraints specified within the design.

The goals and objectives of Service Transition are:

- to enable the business change project or customer to integrate a release into their business processes and services;
- to reduce variations in the predicted and actual performance of the transitioned services;

- to reduce the known errors and minimise the risks from transitioning the service into production;

- to ensure that the service can be used in accordance with the requirements and constraints specified within the service requirements;

- to set customer expectations on how the performance and use of the new or changed service can be used to enable business change;

- to plan and manage the resources to establish successfully a new or changed service into production within the predicted cost, quality and time estimates;

- to ensure there is minimal unpredicted impact on the production services, operations and support organisation;

- to increase the customer, user and Service Management staff satisfaction with the Service Transition practices, including deployment of the new or changed service, communications, release documentation, training and knowledge transfer;

- to increase proper use of the services and underlying applications and technology solutions;

- to provide clear and comprehensive plans that enable the customer and business change projects to align their activities with the Service Transition plans.

SYLLABUS REFERENCE: ITILMD02-6

Understand and explain the main goals and objectives of Service Transition.

Effective Service Transition can significantly improve a service provider's ability to handle a high volume of changes and releases. It enables the service provider to:

- align the new or changed service with the customer's business requirements and business operations;

- ensure that customers and users can use the new or changed service in a way that maximises value to the business operations.

Specifically Service Transition adds value to the business by improving:

- the ability to adapt quickly to new requirements and market developments ('competitive edge');

- transition management of mergers, de-mergers, acquisitions and transfer of services;

- the success rate of changes and releases for the business;

- the predictions of service levels and warranties for new and changed services;

- confidence in the degree of compliance with business and governance requirements during change;

- the variation of actual against estimated and approved resource plans and budgets;

- the productivity of business and customer staff because of better planning and use of new and changed services;

- timely cancellation or changes to maintenance contracts for hardware and software when components are disposed or decommissioned;

- understanding of the level of risk during and after change (e.g. service outage, disruption and rework).

SYLLABUS REFERENCE: ITILMD02-7

Fully comprehend and communicate what value Service Transition provides to the business.

KEY CONCEPTS, DEFINITIONS, PRINCIPLES AND MODELS

The key principles described within this section are:

- Service Transition policy and release policy;

- understanding and communicating transition strategy;

- managing organisational and stakeholder change;

- testing and acceptance criteria and the Service V-model.

Service Transition policy and release policy
A formal policy should be adopted for Service Transition, including:

- **A formal policy for Service Transition:** this should be defined, documented and approved by the management team. This should be communicated throughout the organisation and to all relevant suppliers and partners.

- **Implement all changes to services:** all changes to the Service Portfolio or Service Catalogue should be implemented through Change Management and the changes that are managed by the Service Transition Lifecycle stage are defined and agreed.

- **Adopt a common framework and standards:** Service Transition should be based on a common framework of standard reusable Processes and systems to improve integration of parties involved in Service Transition and reduce variations in the Processes.

- **Maximise reuse of established processes and systems:** Service Transition processes should be aligned with the organisation's Processes and related systems to improve efficiency and effectiveness and where new Processes are required, they should be developed with reuse in mind.

- **Align Service Transition plans with business needs:** Service Transition plans and new or change services should be aligned with the customer and business organisation's requirements in order to maximise value delivered by the change.

- **Establish and maintain relationships with stakeholders:** relationships with customers and customer representatives should be established and maintained throughout Service Transition in order to set their expectations about the new or changed service.

- **Establish effective controls and discipline:** suitable control and disciplines should be established throughout the Service Lifecycle to enable the smooth transition of Service Changes and releases.

- **Provide systems for knowledge transfer and decision support:** systems and Processes should be developed to transfer the knowledge for the effective operation of the service and enable decisions to be made at the right time by competent decision makers

- **Plan release and deployment packages:** release packages should be planned and designed to be built, tested, distributed and deployed into the live environment in a manner that provides the agreed levels of traceability, in a cost-effective and efficient manner.

- **Anticipate and manage course corrections:** staff should be trained to recognise the need for course corrections and be empowered to apply necessary variations within prescribed and understood limits.

- **Proactively manage resources across Service Transitions:** shared and specialist resources should be provided and managed across Service Transition activities to eliminate delays.

- **Ensure early involvement in the Service Lifecycle:** suitable controls and disciplines should be established to check at the earliest possible stage in the Service Lifecycle that a new or changed service will be capable of delivering the value required.

- **Assure the quality of the new or changed service:** the proposed changes to the operational services defined in the service and release definitions, service model and Service Design Package should be verified and validated to ensure that they can deliver the required service requirements and business benefits.

- **Proactively improve quality during Service Transition:** the quality of the new or changed service should be proactively planned and improved.

A formal release policy should also be defined and adopted for one or more services, including:

- the unique identification, numbering and naming conventions for different types of release together with a description;

- the roles and responsibilities at each stage in the release and deployment process;

- the expected frequency for each type of release;

- the approach for accepting and grouping changes into a release;
- the mechanism to automate the build, installation and release distribution processes to improve reuse, repeatability and efficiency;
- how the configuration baseline for the release is captured and verified against the actual release contents;
- exit and entry criteria and authority for acceptance of the release into each Service Transition stage and into the controlled test, training, disaster recovery and production environments;
- criteria and authorisation to exit early life support and handover to Service Operation.

SYLLABUS REFERENCE: ITILMD04-9

Understand and communicate Service Transition Policy and Release policy.

Understanding and communicating transition strategy

Each organisation should develop and adopt a strategy for Service Transition. The Service Transition strategy defines the overall approach to organising and resourcing transitions and should include:

- purpose, goals and objectives of Service Transition;
- context (e.g. service customer, contract portfolios);
- scope (inclusions and exclusions);
- applicable standards, agreements, legal, regulatory and contractual requirements;
- organisations and stakeholders involved in transition;
- framework for Service Transition;
- entry and exit criteria for each release stage;
- identification of requirements and content of the new or changed service;
- people, including roles, responsibilities, training and knowledge;
- approach, including models, plans, evaluation, performance and KPIs;
- deliverables from transition activities, including mandatory and optional documentation for each stage including plans, reports, milestones and budgets.

Communication is crucial to all Service Transition processes. Communications need to be targeted at the right audience and clearly communicate the messages and benefits consistently. Many people are affected by Service Changes. It is important a communications strategy is developed with regard to the contents of communications plans (Figure 7.1).

Figure 7.1 Example of Service Transition communications and plan contents
[Source: OGC ITIL Service Transition ISBN 978-0-113310-48-7]

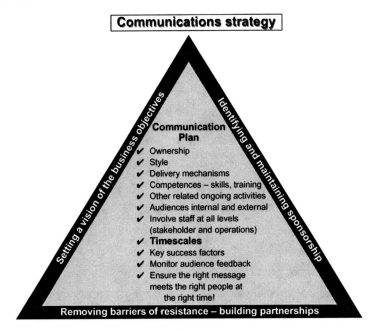

Once a Service Transition communications strategy has been produced it should be used to develop communications plans for all transitions to ensure that stakeholders and interested groups are communicated with effectively and appropriately.

Surveys should be used to measure the effectiveness of Service Transition communications strategy and plans. All feedback should be used to improve all areas of transition communications.

People will be mobilised and engaged if they can see progress. Therefore people need to be kept up to date with the progress of change. Short-term wins should be communicated and progress celebrated.

SYLLABUS REFERENCE: ITILMD04-10

Understand and communicate Transition Strategy.

Managing organisational and stakeholder change
Service Transition's basic role is, on the basis of agreed design, to implement a new or changed service, effectively making the organisation different. Change is an inevitable and important part of organisational development and growth.

Organisational change efforts fail or fall short of their goals because changes and transitions are not led, managed and monitored effectively across the organisation and throughout the change process.

Managing change and transition is the responsibility of the managers and executives involved in change. They must have an awareness that:

- change has to be managed;
- people have to be communicated with openly and honestly;
- resistance has to be sought out, listened to and responded to appropriately.

Organisational change is always a challenge. Factors that drive successful organisational change initiatives include:

- leadership of change;
- organisational culture and adoption;
- governance process;
- organisational capability;
- business and service performance measures;
- strong communication processes with regular opportunity for staff feedback.

For successful Service Transition, an organisation needs to determine the underlying values and drivers that enable the effective management of change. The culture within the organisation can support an implementation or can be the source of resistance to a change. For all major changes an organisational readiness assessment should be completed before implementing the change in order to plan the best approach to the implementation. This is especially true where a change in the sourcing arrangement of the service is being considered. A well-proven approach to managing organisational transformation is to use JP Kotter's *Eight Steps to Transforming your Organisation*.

SYLLABUS REFERENCE: ITILMD04-11

Comprehend how managing organisational and stakeholder change is essential for successful ITSM.

Testing and acceptance criteria and the Service V-model

Release and deployment plans should be linked to the overall Service Transition plans. Release and deployment plans should be authorised through the Change Management process and should define:

- the scope and content of the release;
- a risk assessment and risk profile of the release;

- the organisations and stakeholders affected by the release;
- the stakeholders that approved the change for the release;
- the team responsible for the release;
- the approach to working with stakeholders and deployment groups.

Service Transition is responsible for planning the pass/fail situations for a release. At a minimum these should be defined for each authorisation point through the release and deployment stage. These criteria should be agreed well in advance and published to all stakeholders to set expectations.

The Service V-model (Figure 7.2) can be used to represent and manage the different levels of configuration to be built and tested to deliver service capability:

NB.

Figure 7.2 Service V-model to represent configuration levels and testing (Source: OGC ITIL Service Transition ISBN 978-0-113310-48-7)

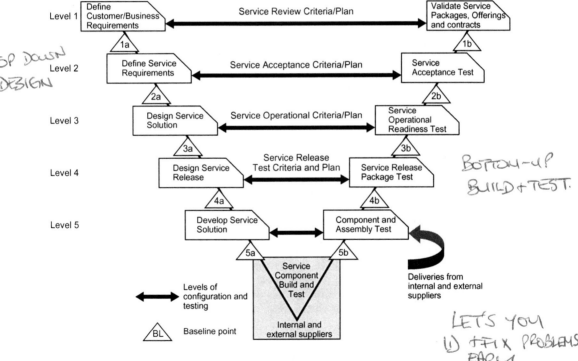

TOP DOWN DESIGN

BOTTOM-UP BUILD + TEST.

LET'S YOU (1) ++IX PROBLEMS EARLY.

The left-hand side of the V represents the specification of the service requirements down to the detailed service design. The right-hand side focuses on the validation and test activities that should be performed against the specifications. This shows

PEOPLE WHO SIGN-OFF DESIGN SHOULD SIGN-OFF TEST.

115

that service validation and acceptance test planning should have a direct involvement with the equivalent party on the left-hand side and start with the definition of the service specification. For example, customers who sign off the agreed service requirements will also sign off the agreed service acceptance criteria and test plan.

The V-model approach is traditionally associated with the waterfall development cycle, but is equally applicable to other lifecycles, such as prototyping and Rapid Application Development (RAD).

A test strategy should be used to define the overall approach to validation and testing, including the organisation of validation and testing activities and resources, and can apply to the whole organisation, a set of services or an individual service.

Various environments will be needed for the different types and levels of testing required. The types of environment required during release and deployment include:

- build environments;
- unit test environments;
- assembly test environments;
- integration test environments;
- system test environments;
- service release test environments;
- Service Operation readiness test environments;
- business simulation environments;
- training environments;
- pilot environments;
- back-up and recovery environments.

Each service model and associated service deliverable is supported by its own reusable test model that can be used for regression testing during the deployment of a specific release, as well as for regression testing of future releases. Test models help with building in quality early within the Service Lifecycle rather than waiting for the results from tests at the end of a release.

SYLLABUS REFERENCE: ITILMD04-12

Explain testing and acceptance criteria and the Service V-model.

Release Units

RELEASE UNIT

Components of an IT service that are normally released together. A Release Unit typically includes sufficient components to perform a useful function.

A Release Unit describes the portions of a service or IT infrastructure that are normally released together according to the organisation's release policy. The Unit may vary depending on the types of component such as hardware or software.

SYLLABUS REFERENCE: ITILMD12-6

Define and explain the Release Unit.

Definitive Media Library

The Definitive Media Library (DML) replaces the Definitive Software Library (DSL) and the Definitive Hardware Store (DHS). The DML is the secure library in which the definitive authorised versions of all media CIs are stored and protected, under the control of Service Asset and Configuration Management (SACM). It stores master copies of versions that have passed quality assurance checks. This library may in reality consist of one or more software libraries or file-storage areas, separate from development, test or live file-storage areas. It contains the master copies of all controlled software in an organisation. The DML should include definitive copies of purchased software (along with licence documents or information), as well as software developed on site. Master copies of controlled documentation for a system are also stored in the DML in electronic form.

An area should also be set aside for the secure storage of definitive hardware spares. These are spare components and assemblies that are maintained at the same level as the comparative systems within the controlled test or live environment. Details of these components, their locations and their respective builds and contents should be comprehensively recorded in the CMS. These can then be used in a controlled manner when needed for additional systems or in the recovery from incidents. Once their (temporary) use has ended, they are returned to the spares store or replacements are obtained.

The relationship between the DML and CMS is shown in Figure 7.3.

SYLLABUS REFERENCE: ITILMD12-3

Define and explain the Definitive Media Library.

Figure 7.3 The relationship between the DML and the CMS (Source: OGC ITIL Service Transition ISBN 978-0-113310-48-7)

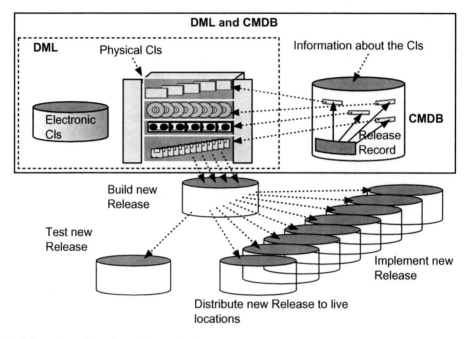

Models and options for release deployment

There are many different options for deploying new releases, including:

- release and deployment options;
- release and deployment models.

Release and deployment options
Big bang versus phased

- **Big bang:** the new or changed service is deployed to all user areas in one operation. This will often be used when introducing an application change and consistency of service across the organisation is considered important.

- **Phased:** the service is deployed to a part of the user base initially, and then this operation is repeated for subsequent parts of the user base via a scheduled roll-out plan. This will be the case in many scenarios such as in retail organisations for new services being introduced into the stores' environment in manageable phases.

Push versus pull

- **Push** approaches are used where the service component is deployed from the centre and pushed out to the target locations. In terms of service deployment, delivering updated service components to all users, either in big-bang or phased form, constitutes 'push', since the new or changed service is delivered into the users' environment at a time not of their choosing.

- **Pull** approaches are used for software releases where the software is made available in a central location but users are free to pull the software down to their own location at a time of their choosing or when a user workstation restarts. The use of 'pull' updating a release over the internet has made this concept significantly more pervasive.

Automated versus manual

- **Automation** will help to ensure repeatability and consistency. The time required to provide a well-designed and efficient automated mechanism may not always be available or viable.

- When a **manual** mechanism is used, it is important to monitor and measure the impact of many repeated manual activities because they are likely to be inefficient and error-prone. Too many manual activities will slow down the release team and create resource or capacity issues that affect the service levels. Manual release mechanisms would have to be used if a new desktop release was required that included both hardware and software updates.

Release and deployment models

Release and deployment models are used by Service Design to select the most appropriate approach to the deployment of releases to the live environment. Release and deployment models define:

- release structure – the overall structure for building a release package and the target environments;
- the exit and entry criteria, including mandatory and optional deliverables and documentation for each stage;
- controlled environments that are required to build and test the release for each release level;
- the roles and responsibilities for each configuration item at each release level;
- the release promotion and configuration baseline model;
- template release and deployment schedules;
- supporting systems, tools and procedures for documenting and tracking all release and deployment activities;
- the handover activities and responsibilities for executing the handover and acceptance for each stage of release and deployment.

PROCESSES

The main Processes within the Service Transition stage of the Lifecycle are:

- Transition Planning and Support;
- Change Management*;
- Service Asset and Configuration Management*;

- Release and Deployment Management;
- Service Validation and Testing;
- Evaluation;
- Knowledge Management.

The two Processes identified with an asterisk were contained in ITIL v2 and only the changes have been covered within this section. There were changes made to the Change Management process with regards to Service Changes and change types. The other five areas are considered in more detail.

Transition Planning and Support
Purpose, goal, objectives and scope
The purpose of the Transition Planning and Support activities is to:

- plan appropriate capacity and resources to package a release, build, release, test, deploy and establish the new or changed service into production;
- provide support for the Service Transition teams and people;
- plan the changes required in a manner that ensures the integrity of all identified customer assets, service assets and configurations can be maintained as they evolve through Service Transition;
- ensure that Service Transition issues, risks and deviations are reported to the appropriate stakeholders and decision makers;
- coordinate activities across projects, suppliers and service teams where required.

The goals of Transition Planning and Support are:

- to plan and coordinate the resources to ensure that the requirements of Service Strategy encoded in Service Design are effectively realised in Service Operation;
- to identify, manage and control the risks of failure and disruption across transition activities.

The objectives of Transition Planning and Support are:

- to plan and coordinate the resources to establish successfully a new or changed service into production within the predicted cost, quality and time estimates;
- to ensure that all parties adopt the common framework of standard reusable processes and supporting systems in order to improve the effectiveness and efficiency of the integrated planning and coordination activities;
- to provide clear and comprehensive plans that enable the customer and business change projects to align their activities with the Service Transition plans.

The scope of the Service Transition Planning and Support activities includes:

- incorporating design and operation requirements into the transition plans;
- managing and operating Transition Planning and Support activities;
- maintaining and integrating Service Transition plans across the customer, service and contract portfolios;
- managing Service Transition progress, changes, issues, risks and deviations;
- quality review of all Service Transition, release and deployment plans;
- managing and operating the transition processes, supporting systems and tools;
- communications with customers, users and stakeholders;
- monitoring and improving Service Transition performance.

Service Design will develop a Service Design Package (SDP, see Chapter 4) that will be provided to Service Transition to guide the new or changed service through transition and the remainder of its lifecycle.

The Transition Planning and Support activities
The Transition and Support process should consist of the following activities.

Service Transition and Release policies
A Transition Policy and a Release Policy should be produced. The content of these have been discussed earlier in this chapter.

All releases should have a unique identifier that can be used by Configuration Management. A release is a collection of new or changed components required to implement one or more changes. The types of release should be agreed. Typical examples are:

- **Major releases:** normally contain large areas of new functionality.
- **Minor releases:** normally containing small enhancements and fixes.
- **Emergency releases:** normally used to resolve critical business requirements.

A release policy would specify the use and frequency of such releases, for example only critical 'emergency releases' will be released between formally scheduled releases.

Prepare for Service Transition
There are a number of preparation activities that should be completed before starting a transition, including:

- reviewing and accepting of inputs from the other Service Lifecycle stages;
- reviewing and checking the input deliverables (e.g. SDP, SAC and evaluation report);

- identifying, raising and scheduling Requests for Change (RFC);
- checking that the configuration baselines are recorded in Configuration Management before the start of Service Transition;
- checking transition readiness.

Planning and coordinating Service Transition

Once the preparation activities have been completed the transition, planning and coordinating activities should be started including:

- planning an individual transition;
- integrated planning;
- adopting programme and project management practices;
- reviewing the plans.

Advice and administration

Transition Support and Planning should provide support for all stakeholders to understand and be able to follow the Service Transition framework of processes and supporting systems and tools.

The process should also provide administration for managing changes and work orders, issues, risks deviations and waivers, tools and Processes. It should also provide stakeholder communication and monitoring of transition performance.

Progress monitoring and reporting

Monitoring and reporting activities should monitor progress against intentions as set out in the transition model and plans. They will subsequently establish if the transition is proceeding to plan.

Process KPIs and challenges

Some of the primary KPIs of the Transition Support and Planning process that should be considered for measuring the effectiveness of the activities are:

- the number of releases implemented that met the customer's agreed requirements in terms of cost, quality, scope and release schedule (expressed as a percentage of all releases);
- reduced variation of actual against predicted scope, quality, cost and time;
- increased customer and user satisfaction with plans and communications that enable the business to align their activities with Service Transition plans;
- reduction in the number of issues, risks and delays caused by inadequate planning.

The challenges facing the Transition Support and Planning process are:

- continually changing business needs;
- gaining appropriate involvement, support and buy-in of key business personnel and management;

- maintaining alignment between the business transition plans and activities and IT transition plans and activities;

- resistance to change.

Release and Deployment Management

The purpose of Release and Deployment Management activities is:

- to define and agree release and deployment plans with customers and stakeholders;

- to ensure that each Release Package consists of a set of related assets and service components that are compatible with each other;

- to ensure that integrity of a release package and its constituent components is maintained throughout the transition activities and recorded accurately in the CMS;

- to ensure that all release and deployment packages can be tracked, installed, tested, verified and/or uninstalled or backed out if appropriate;

- to ensure that organisation and stakeholder change is managed during the release and deployment activities;

- to record and manage deviations, risks, issues related to the new or changed service and take necessary corrective action;

- to ensure that there is knowledge transfer to enable the customers and users to optimise their use of the service to support their business activities;

- to ensure that skills and knowledge are transferred to operations and support staff to enable them to effectively and efficiently deliver, support and maintain the service according to required warranties and service levels.

The goal of Release and Deployment Management is to deploy releases into production and establish effective use of the service in order to deliver value to the customer and be able to handover to Service Operation.

The objectives of Release and Deployment Management are to ensure that:

- there are clear and comprehensive release and deployment plans that enable the customer and business change projects to align their activities with these plans;

- release packages can be built, installed, tested and deployed efficiently to deployment groups or target environments successfully and on schedule;

- new or changed services and their enabling systems, technology and organisation are capable of delivering the agreed service requirements (i.e. Utilities, Warranties and Service Levels);

- there is minimal unpredicted impact on the production services, operations and support organisation;

- customers, users and Service Management staff are satisfied with the Service Transition practices and outputs.

The scope of Release and Deployment Management includes the Processes, systems and functions to package, build, test and deploy a release into production and establish the service specified in the Service Design package before final handover to Service Operation.

The Release and Deployment Management process should consist of the following activities.

Planning

Planning activities should include:

- production of release and deployment plans, containing:

    - scope and content of the release;

    - risk assessment and risk profile for the release;

    - organisations and stakeholders affected by the release;

    - stakeholders that approved the change request for the release and/or deployment;

    - team responsible for the release;

    - approach to working with stakeholders and deployment groups.

- pass and fail criteria for release and deployment;

- build and test prior to production;

- planning pilots;

- planning release packaging and build;

- deployment planning;

- logistics and delivery planning;

- financial and commercial planning.

Preparation for build, test and deployment

The service design and the release design must be validated against the requirements before being authorised.

Build and test

Build and test should include:

- management of service and infrastructure configurations;

- release and build documentation;

- acquire and test input configuration items and components;

- release packaging;

- build and manage test environments.

Service testing and pilots

Testing should include:

- deployment readiness test;
- service rehearsals;
- pilots.

Plan and prepare for deployment

- assessment;
- develop plans and prepare for deployment.

Perform transfer, deployment and retirement

- transfer financial assets;
- transition business and organisation;
- deploy Processes and materials.
- transfer service;
- deploy service;
- decommission and service retirement;
- remove redundant assets.

Verify deployment

Check and verify that all users, Service Operation and all other stakeholders and interested parties are capable of using or operating the service.

Early life support

This provides appropriate resources and skills to resolve operational and support issues promptly, wherever required to support business activities without unwanted disruption.

Review and close deployment

Review targets, achievements, any quality issues and lessons learnt and produce reports and feedback.

Review and close Service Transition

A formal review and closure, checking all activities, actions and documents are complete.

Process KPIs and challenges

Some of the main KPIs of the Release and Deployment Management process that should be considered for measuring the effectiveness of the activities include:

- From the customer or business perspective:

  - Variance from service performance required by customers (minimal and reducing).

  - Number of incidents against the service (low and reducing).

  - Increased customer and user satisfaction with the services delivered.

  - Decreased customer dissatisfaction. Service issues resulting from poorly tested or untested services increases the negative perception on the service provider organisation as a whole.

- From the service provider perspective:

  - Reduced resources and costs to diagnose and fix incidents and problems in deployment and production.

  - Increased adoption of the Service Transition common framework of standards, reusable Processes and supporting documentation.

  - Reduced discrepancies in configuration audits compared with the real world.

The challenges facing the Release and Deployment Management process include:

- developing standard performance measures and measurement methods across projects and suppliers;
- dealing with projects and suppliers where estimated delivery dates are inaccurate and there are delays in scheduling Service Transition activities;
- understanding the different stakeholder perspectives that underpin effective risk management for the change impact assessment and test activities;
- building a thorough understanding of risks that have impacted or may impact successful Service Transition of services and releases;
- encouraging a risk management culture where people share information and take a pragmatic and measured approach to risk.

Service Validation and Testing
Purpose, goal, objectives and scope
The purpose of Service Validation and Testing activities is:

- to plan and implement a structured validation and test process that provides objective evidence that the new or changed service will support the customer's business and stakeholder requirements, including the agreed service levels;
- to quality assure a release, its constituent service components, the resultant service and service capability delivered by a release;
- to identify, assess and address issues, errors and risks throughout Service Transition.

The goal of Service Validation and Testing is to assure that a service will provide value to customers and their business.

The objectives of Service Validation and Testing are:

- to provide confidence that a release will create a new or changed service that delivers the expected outcomes and value for the customers within the projected costs, capacity and constraints;
- to validate that a service is 'fit for purpose':

  - delivering the required performance with desired constraints removed;
  - by meeting the agreed specifications under the specified terms and conditions of use.

- to confirm that the customer and stakeholder requirements for the new or changed service are correctly defined and remedy any errors or variances early in the Service Lifecycle.

The scope of Service Validation and Testing should apply to in-house or externally developed or provided services, and be applied throughout the Service Lifecycle to quality assure any aspect of a service and the service providers' capability, resources and capacity to deliver a service. The output from testing is used by the Evaluate process to provide the information to independently judge whether the service will deliver service performance with an acceptable risk profile.

The Service Validation and Testing activities

Service assurance is delivered though verification and validation, which in turn are delivered through testing (trying something out in conditions that represent the final live situation – a test environment) and by observation or review against a standard or specification.

The Service Validation and Testing process should consist of the following activities.

Service quality and assurance

Service quality and assurance are the completion of:

- **Validation:** confirmation through the provision of objective evidence that the requirements for a specific intended use or application have been fulfilled.
- **Verification:** confirmation through the provision of objective evidence that specific requirements have been fulfilled.
- **Use of policies:** the following policies are available and are used appropriately:

  - Service quality policy;
  - Risk policy;

- Service Transition Policy;
- Release policy;
- Change Management policy;

- **Use of a test strategy:** a test strategy is available, used and includes:

  - purpose, goals and objectives of service testing and context;
  - applicable standards, legal and regulatory requirements;
  - applicable contracts, agreements and policies for testing;
  - scope, organisations and teams;
  - test processes;
  - test metrics and improvement;
  - identification of items to be tested;
  - Service Operation plan;
  - Service Management plans;
  - service provider interfaces;
  - approach;
  - criteria;
  - people requirements, roles and responsibilities;
  - deliverables and reports.

Use of test models
The use of a test model including a test plan, what is to be tested and the test scripts that define how each element will be tested. A test model ensures that testing is executed consistently in a repeatable way that is effective and efficient. The test scripts define the release test conditions, associated expected results and test cycles.

Validation and testing perspectives
These focus on whether the service will perform as required, from the perspective of those who will use, deliver, deploy, manage and operate the service. The test entry and exit criteria are developed as the SDP develops.

Levels of testing and test models
These are derived from the design and build of the system and service and are often related to a test model. Test models help in building quality into a service or system early in the Service Lifecycle. The V-model maps the types of test required at each stage of the development of the service.

Testing approaches and techniques
The type of testing used for each service will depend on the type of service, the Service Model, risk profiles, skill levels and levels of testing, and may include:

- document review;
- modelling and measuring;
- a risk-based approach that focuses on areas of greatest risk;
- a standards compliance approach;
- an experience-based approach;
- an approach based on an organisation's lifecycle methods (e.g. waterfall, agile);
- simulation;
- scenario testing;
- role playing;
- prototyping;
- laboratory testing;
- regression testing;
- joint walkthrough/workshops;
- dress/service rehearsal;
- conference room pilot;
- live pilot.

All of these aspects are used within a set of validation and testing activities as shown in Figure 7.4.

Figure 7.4 Example of a validation and testing process (Source: OGC ITIL Service Transition ISBN 978-0-113310-48-7)

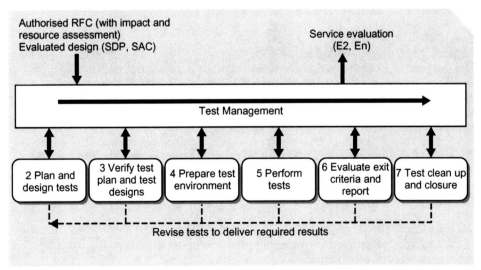

Process KPIs and challenges

Some of the main KPIs of the Release and Deployment Management process that should be considered for measuring the effectiveness of the activities are:

- an early validation that the service will deliver the predicted value that enables early correction;
- a reduction in the impact of incidents and errors when live that are attributable to newly transitioned services;
- a more effective use of resource and involvement from the customer/business;
- reduced delays in testing that impact the business;
- an increased mutual understanding of the new or changed service;
- a clear understanding of roles and responsibilities associated with the new or changed service between the customers, users and service provider;
- cost and resources required from user and customer involvement.

The challenges facing the Service Validation and Testing process are:

- an inability to maintain test environment and test data that matches the live environment;
- insufficient staff, skills and testing tools to deliver adequate testing coverage;
- projects overrunning and allocated testing time frames being squeezed to restore project go-live dates but at the cost of quality;
- developing standard performance measures and measurement methods across projects and suppliers;
- projects and suppliers estimating delivery dates inaccurately and causing delays in scheduling Service Transition activities.

Evaluation

Purpose, goal, objectives and scope

The purpose of Evaluation activities is to provide a consistent and standardised means of determining the performance of a Service Change in the context of existing and proposed services and IT infrastructure. The actual performance of a change is assessed against its predicted performance and any deviations between the two are understood and managed.

The goal of Evaluation is to set stakeholder expectations correctly and provide effective and accurate information to Change Management.

The objectives of Evaluation are:

- to evaluate the intended effects of a Service Change and as much of the unintended effects as is reasonably practical given capacity, resource and organisational constraints;

- to provide good quality outputs from the evaluation process so that Change Management can expedite an effective decision about whether a Service Change is to be approved.

The scope of the Evaluation activities includes an Evaluation assessment of the suitability of new or changed services defined by Service Design, during the deployment and before final transition to Service Operation. The importance of evaluating the actual performance of any Service Change against its anticipated performance is an important source of information to service providers to help ensure that realistic expectations are set and to identify any service performance limitations.

The Evaluation activities

The Evaluation process should consist of the following activities:

- **Plan the evaluation:** the evaluation should be planned and should include the understanding of both intended effects and unintended effects and the specific measures that should be used to evaluate theses effects.

- **Evaluate predicted performance:** a risk assessment is completed using customer requirements and the predicted performance model. If the assessment indicates that risks are associated with the predicted performance, then an interim report should be sent to Change Management.

- **Evaluate actual performance:** once the change has been implemented another risk assessment is completed and, if the level of risk is unacceptable, another interim report should be sent to Change Management.

- **Evaluation reporting:** evaluation reports should be produced containing risk profiles, deviation reports, a qualification statement, a validation statement and a set of recommendations.

The flow between these activities is shown in Figure 7.5.

Process KPIs and challenges

Some of the main KPIs of the Evaluation process that should be considered for measuring the effectiveness of the activities are:

- reducing variance from service performance required by customers;
- reducing number of incidents against the service;
- reducing cycle time to perform an evaluation;
- the number of failed designs that have been transitioned (zero).

The challenges facing the Evaluation process are:

- developing standard performance measures and measurement methods across projects and suppliers;
- projects and suppliers estimating delivery dates inaccurately and causing delays in scheduling evaluation activities;

Figure 7.5 The Evaluation process (Source: OGC ITIL Service Transition ISBN 978-0-113310-48-7)

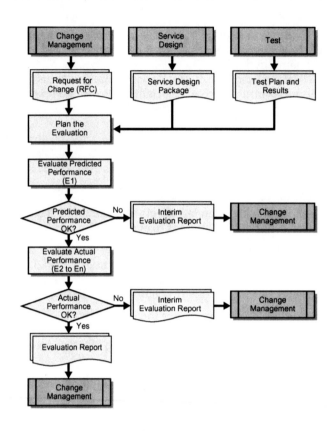

- understanding the different stakeholder perspectives that underpin effective risk management for the evaluation activities;
- understanding, and being able to assess, the balance between managing risk and taking risks as it affects the overall strategy of the organisation and service delivery;
- measuring and demonstrating less variation in predictions during and after transition;
- taking a pragmatic and measured approach to risk;
- communicating the organisation's attitude to risk and approach to risk management effectively during risk evaluation;
- building a thorough understanding of risks that have impacted or may impact successful Service Transition of services and releases;
- encouraging a risk management culture where people share information.

Knowledge Management
Purpose, goal, objectives and scope

The purpose of Knowledge Management activities is to ensure that the right information is delivered to the appropriate place or competent person at the right time to enable informed decisions.

The goal of Knowledge Management is to enable organisations to improve the quality of management decision-making by ensuring that reliable and secure information and data is available throughout the Service Lifecycle.

The objectives of Knowledge Management include:

- enabling the service provider to be more efficient and improve quality of service, increase satisfaction and reduce the cost of service;
- ensuring staff have a clear and common understanding of the value that their services provide to customers and the ways in which benefits are realised from the use of those services;
- ensuring that, at a given time and location, service provider staff have adequate information on services and their usage.

The scope of the Knowledge Management process extends across the whole Service Lifecycle in that it is relevant to all Lifecycle sectors and hence is referenced throughout ITIL. Knowledge Management includes the information and the data from which the knowledge derives.

The Knowledge Management process should consist of the following activities:

The Data → Information → Knowledge → Wisdom structure

Knowledge Management typically consists of the Data → Information → Knowledge → Wisdom (DIKW) structure shown in Figure 7.6.

- **Data:** a set of discrete facts about events. Most organisations capture significant amounts of information about events. The key Knowledge Management activities concerned with data are the identification of the relevant data, the capture of accurate data and its analysis into information.
- **Information:** comes from providing context to data. The key Knowledge Management activities concerned with information are managing the content in a way that makes it easy to query, find, reuse and learn from experiences.
- **Knowledge:** composed of the tacit experiences, ideas, insights, values and judgements of individuals. Knowledge puts information into an 'ease of use' format which helps decision-making.
- **Wisdom:** gives the ultimate discernment of material together with the application and contextual awareness to provide a strong common sense judgement.

Figure 7.6 The flow from data to wisdom (Source: OGC ITIL Service Transition ISBN 978-0-113310-48-7)

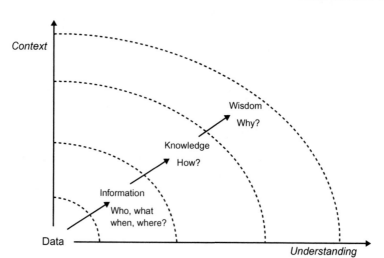

The maintenance of a Service Knowledge Management Systems (SKMS)
The structure and content of the SKMS was discussed in Chapter 4. The SKMS underpins the operation of all Knowledge Management activities. The maintenance of a well-structured and easily accessible SKMS is key to a successful Knowledge Management process.

Creation of a Knowledge Management strategy
This strategy should identify and plan for the capture of the knowledge and the consequential data and information that will support it. The strategy should address:

- the governance model;
- organisational changes underway, and planned and consequential changes in roles and responsibilities;
- establishing roles and responsibilities and ongoing funding;
- policies, processes, procedures and methods for:
  - Knowledge Management;
  - technology and other resource requirements;
  - performance measures.

Knowledge transfer
The challenge is often the practical problem of getting knowledge from one part of the organisation to other parts of the organisation. Knowledge transfer is very complex and it is essential that the information is made available in

an 'easy to use' manner and is structured and formatted according to those trying to access it. The success of a Knowledge Management process is often determined by the ease and accessibility of the SKMS and its information.

Management of data and information

Knowledge rests on the management of the information and data that underpins it. Management of data and information includes:

- establishing data and information requirements;
- defining the information architecture;
- establishing data and information management procedures;
- evaluation and improvement.

Using the SKMS

The provision of consistent quality and support of services across support groups, time zones, working practices and geographies requires good sharing of information and knowledge throughout all areas of the organisation. Implementation and use of an effective SKMS helps reduce the cost of maintaining services and improves the consistency of service delivery.

Process KPIs and challenges

Some of the main KPIs of the Knowledge Management process that should be considered for measuring the effectiveness of the activities are:

- successful implementation and early-life operation of new and changed services with few knowledge-related errors;
- increased responsiveness to changing business demands (e.g. higher percentage of queries and questions solved via single access to internet/ intranet through use of search and index systems such as Google®);
- improved accessibility and management of standards and policies;
- improved knowledge dissemination;
- reduced time and effort required to support and maintain services;
- reduced time to find information for diagnosis and fixing incidents and problems;
- reduced dependency on personnel for knowledge.

The challenges facing the Knowledge Management process are:

- creating a 'knowledge-sharing culture';
- identifying the relevant data and information;
- the implementation of a simple and effective system and process for knowledge sharing and information and knowledge retrieval;
- persuading staff to share key information and knowledge.

Change Management changes

The three major changes in area of Change Management process are:

- Service Changes;
- change types;
- the Seven Rs of Change Management.

These are explained in the following sections.

Service changes

Change can be defined in many ways.

SERVICE CHANGE

The addition, modification or removal of authorised, planned or a supported service or service component and its associated documentation.

The scope of Change Management covers changes to baseline service assets and configuration items across the whole Service Lifecycle. Each organisation should define the changes that lie outside the scope of their Service Change process. Typically these might include:

- changes with significantly wider impacts than Service Changes (e.g. departmental organisation, policies and business operations) that would produce RFCs to generate consequential Service Changes;
- changes at an operational level, such as repair to printers or other routine service components.

Change types

There are three types of change: Normal change, Standard change and Emergency change.

NORMAL CHANGE

A change that follows normal change procedures.

STANDARD CHANGE

A pre-approved change that is low risk, relatively common and follows a procedure or work instruction. For example password reset or provision of standard equipment to a new employee. RFCs are not required to implement a Standard change, and they are logged and tracked using a different mechanism, such as a Service Request.

EMERGENCY CHANGE

A change that must be introduced as soon as possible. For example to resolve a Major Incident or implement a security patch. The Change Management process will normally have a specific procedure for handling emergency changes.

- Normal changes include changes to the Service Portfolio, to a service or a service definition, a project change proposal, user access request or operational activity.

- A Standard change is a low risk, relatively common change to a service or infrastructure component(s) for which the approach is pre-authorised by Change Management and there is an accepted and established procedure to provide a specific change requirement. Examples might include new starters within an organisation, or a desktop move for a single user.

- Emergency changes are normally reserved for resolution of business critical situations. The number of Emergency changes should be kept to a minimum because they are disruptive and more likely to fail.

The seven Rs of Change Management
The following questions must be answered for all changes. Without this information, the impact assessment cannot be completed, and the balance of risk and benefit to the live service will not be understood. This could result in the change not delivering all the possible or expected business benefits or even of it having a detrimental, unexpected effect on the live service.

- Who **raised** the change?
- What is the **reason** for the change?
- What is the **return** required from the change?
- What are the **risks** involved in the change?
- What **resources** are required to deliver the change?
- Who is **responsible** for the build, test and implementation of the change?
- What is the **relationship** between this change and other changes?

SYLLABUS REFERENCE: ITILMD13-3

Understand the changes made at ITIL v3 to specific parts of Change Management.

ROLES, RESPONSIBILITIES AND FUNCTIONS

The main additional new roles, responsibilities and functions associated with Service Transition are detailed below.

Roles
Service Transition Manager
The Service Transition manager has day-to-day management and control of the Service Transition teams and their activities. The responsibilities include:

- overall planning and management of Service Transition delivery including Continual Service Improvement;

- managing and coordinating the Service Transition functions;

- budgeting and accounting for Service Transition team activities and resources;

- acting as the prime interface for senior management in terms of Service Transition planning and reporting;

- making a final recommendation to the business and IT regarding the decisions to release and deploy into production;

- ensuring all organisational policies and procedures are followed throughout transition;

- ensuring the final delivery meets the agreed customer and stakeholder requirements specified in the Service Design.

Performance Risk and Evaluation Manager
The Performance Risk and Evaluation Manager responsibilities include:

- using Service Design and Release package to develop the evaluation plan to input to service testing;

- establishing risks and issues associated with all aspects of the Service Transition through risk workshops etc.;

- providing evaluation reports to input to Change Management.

Knowledge Management Manager Process Owner
The Knowledge Management Process Owner's responsibilities include:

- undertaking the Knowledge Management role, ensuring compliance with the organisation's policies and processes;

- being the architect of knowledge identification, capture and maintenance;

- identifying, controlling and storing any information deemed to be pertinent to the services provided, which is not available via any other means;

- maintaining the controlled knowledge items to ensure currency;
- ensuring all knowledge items are made accessible to those who need them in an efficient and effective manner;
- monitoring publicity regarding the knowledge information to ensure that information is not duplicated and is recognised as a central source of information etc.;
- acting as an adviser to business and IT personnel on Knowledge Management matters, including policy decisions on storage, value, worth etc.

Service Test Manager

The Service Test Manager is primarily responsible for the test support and test team functions and is responsible for:

- defining the Test Strategy;
- designing and planning test conditions, test scripts and test data sets to ensure appropriate and adequate coverage and control;
- allocating and overseeing test resources, ensuring test policies are adhered to;
- providing management reporting on test progress, test outcomes, success rates, issues and risks;
- conducting tests as defined in the test plans and design;
- recording, analysing, diagnosing, reporting and managing test events, Incidents, Problems and retesting dependent on agreed criteria;
- managing test environment requirements;
- verifying tests conducted by release and deployment teams;
- administering test assets and components.

Release and Deployment Manager

The Release and Deployment Manager is responsible for the planning, design, build, configuration and testing of all software and hardware to create the release package for the delivery of, or changes to, the designated service including:

- managing all aspects of the end-to-end release process;
- updating the SKMS and CMS;
- ensuring coordination of build and test environment team and release teams;
- ensuring teams follow the organisation's established policies and procedures;
- providing management reports on release progress;
- service release and deployment policy and planning;
- release package design, build and configuration;
- release package acceptance including business sign-off;

- service roll-out planning including method of deployment;
- release package testing to predefined Acceptance Criteria;
- signing-off the release package for implementation;
- release and deployment communication, preparation and training;
- auditing hardware and software before and after the implementation of release package changes;
- installing new or upgraded hardware;
- storage and traceability/auditability of controlled software in both centralised and distributed systems;
- release, distribution and the installation of packaged software.

Release Packaging and Build Manager
The Release Packaging and Build Manager has the following responsibilities:

- establishing the final release configuration (e.g. knowledge, information, hardware, software and infrastructure);
- building the final release delivery;
- testing the final delivery prior to independent testing;
- establishing and reporting outstanding known errors and workarounds;
- providing input to the final implementation sign-off process;
- liaising with all other process areas on their requirements.

Early-life support
Early-life support should be considered as an integral role within the release and deployment phase, with staff having the following responsibilities:

- to provide IT service and business functional support from prior to final acceptance by Service Operation;
- to ensure delivery of appropriate support documentation;
- to provide release acceptance for provision of initial support;
- to provide initial support in response to Incidents and errors detected within a new or changed service;
- to adapt and perfect elements that evolve with initial usage, such as embedding activities for a new or changed service;
- to deal with formal transition of the service to Service Operation and CSI;
- to monitor Incidents and Problems, and to undertake Problem Management during release and deployment, raising RFCs as required;
- to provide initial performance reporting and undertake service risk assessment based on performance.

Deployment staff
Deployment staff have the following responsibilities:

- to deal with the final physical delivery of the service implementation;
- to coordinate release documentation and communications, including training, customer, Service Management and technical release notes;
- to plan the deployment in conjunction with Change and Knowledge Management and SACM;
- to provide technical and application guidance and support throughout the release process, including known errors and workarounds;
- to provide feedback on the effectiveness of the release;
- to record metrics for deployment to ensure compliance with agreed SLAs.

Functions
Planning and support
Planning and support may not be a direct responsibility of the Service Transition Manager because in some organisations this function may be consolidated into an overall Service Management office/IT planning responsibility. Regardless of where this function sits, the role must still be performed. This function provides support for the Service Transition teams and people. The activities include:

- defining the requirements, Processes and tools for Transition Planning and Support;
- maintaining and integrating lower level plans to establish overall integrated transition plans, including planned versus actuals;
- maintaining and monitoring progress on Service Transition changes, issues, risks and deviations including tracking progress on actions and mitigation of risks;
- maintaining records on and providing management information on resource usage, project/Service Transition progress, budgeted and actual spend;
- managing and coordinating requests for resources;
- coordinating Service Transition activities across projects, suppliers and service teams where appropriate;
- publishing Service Transition performance statistics and identifying key areas for improvement;
- undertaking formal quality reviews of the Service Transition, release and deployment plans and agreed transition;
- managing support for tools and Service Transition processes;
- communicating with stakeholders.

Test Support team
The prime responsibility of the test support team function is to provide independent testing of all components delivered within the Service Transition

programme or project. Responsibilities required to deliver successful service testing include the following, however, not all of these are the direct responsibility of the Test Support team:

- Test analysts carry out the tests as set out in the test plans and/or service package.

- Liaising with the Change Manager, who is responsible for ensuring that tests are developed appropriate to approved changes and that the agreed testing strategy and policy is applied.

- Liaising with the relevant developers/suppliers responsible for establishing the root cause of test failures: the fault in the service component that made the test fail.

- Liaising with Service Design who are responsible for designing tests. This will generally involve the use of standard transition and testing models.

- Liaising with customers and users to ensure that the appropriate testing is completed.

Build and Test Environment Management

The Build and Test Environment function is primarily to ensure that all the relevant people have the appropriate environments, test data, versioned software etc. available at the time that they need it and for the right purpose. Environment resources are normally limited so this function performs a coordinating and sometimes arbitrary role to ensure that resources are used to maximum effect. Build and Test Environment staff have the following key responsibilities:

- Ensuring service infrastructure and applications are built to the design specification.

- Planning acquisition, build, implementation and maintenance of ICT infrastructure.

- Ensuring build delivery components are from controlled sources.

- Developing an integrated application software and infrastructure build.

- Delivering appropriate build, operations and support documentation for the build and test environments prior to handover to Service Operation.

- Building, delivering and maintaining required testing environments.

SYLLABUS REFERENCE: ITILMD05-4a

Explain the objectives, scope, concepts, activities, key metrics, roles and challenges for Transition Planning and Support, Release and Deployment Management.

8 SERVICE OPERATION

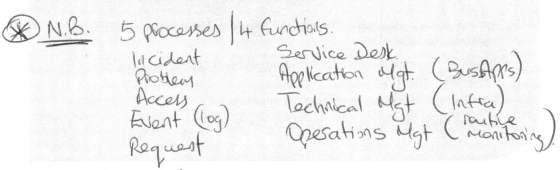

Ⓧ N.B. 5 processes | 4 functions.
Incident   Service Desk.
Problem   Application Mgt. (BusApps)
Access   Technical Mgt (Infra)
Event (log)   Operations Mgt (routine monitoring)
Request

know defs:

LEARNING OBJECTIVES

The purpose of this chapter is to help candidates understand all aspects of the Service Operation stage of the Lifecycle, including:

- the purpose, goals, objectives and value;
- the key concepts, definitions, principles and models;
- the Processes;
- the roles, responsibilities and functions.

N.B. ⓧ **PURPOSE, GOALS, OBJECTIVES AND VALUE**

The purpose of Service Operation is to coordinate and carry out the activities and Processes required to deliver and manage services at agreed levels to business users and customers. Service Operation is also responsible for the ongoing management of the technology that is used to deliver and support services.

Well-designed and well-implemented Processes will be of little value if the day-to-day operation of those Processes is not properly conducted, controlled and managed. Also, service improvements can be impossible if day-to-day activities to monitor performance, assess metrics and gather data are not systematically conducted during Service Operation.

SYLLABUS REFERENCE: ITILMD02-8

Understand and explain the main goals and objectives of Service Operation.

The Operation stage is where the plans, designs and optimisation of services are executed and measured. From a customer viewpoint, Service Operation is where actual value is realised. The true business value can be obtained when:

- the services are operated within the budgetary and ROI targets established earlier in the Lifecycle;
- design or transition flaws or unforeseen requirements are resolved with all operational services;
- the efficiency of Service Operation is improved;
- the performance of operational services is optimised.

SYLLABUS REFERENCE: ITILMD02-9

Fully comprehend and communicate what value Service Operation provides to the business.

KEY CONCEPTS, DEFINITIONS, PRINCIPLES AND MODELS

The key principles described within this section are:

- achieving balance in Service Operation;
- self-help;
- event types.

Achieving balance in Service Operation

Service Operation is more than just execution of a standard set of procedures or activities. It has to deal with an ever-changing environment which results in a conflict between maintaining the status quo and adapting to continual changes to the business and technical environments.

There are four main areas where Service Operation has to balance these conflicting demands.

Achieving balance between internal and external focus

The most fundamental conflict in all the phases of the Service Lifecycle is between the view of IT as a set of IT services, from the external business perspective, and the view of IT as a set of technology components, the internal IT perspective (Figure 8.1).

- The external view of IT is the way in which services are experienced by its users and customers.
- The internal view of IT is the way in which IT components and systems are managed to deliver the services.

Both of these views are necessary when delivering services. The organisation that focuses on business requirements alone without thinking about how they are going to be delivered will end up making promises that cannot be kept. The organisation that focuses on internal systems alone without thinking about what services they support will end up with expensive services that deliver little value.

(✱) There are TENSION METRICS

Figure 8.1 Achieving a balance between external and internal focus (Source: OGC ITIL Service Operation ISBN 978-0-113310-46-3)

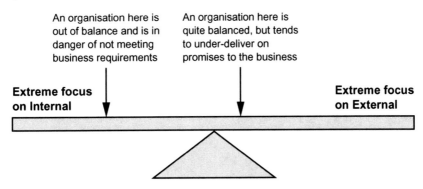

Achieving balance between focus on stability and responsiveness
No matter how good the functionality of an IT service is and no matter how well it has been designed, it will be worth far less if the service components are not available or if they perform inconsistently. This means that Service Operation needs to ensure that the IT infrastructure is stable and available as designed. At the same time, Service Operation needs to recognise that business and IT requirements change (Figure 8.2).

Figure 8.2 Achieving a balance between focus on stability and responsiveness (Source: OGC ITIL Service Operation ISBN 978-0-113310-46-3)

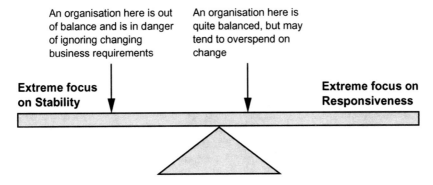

Some of these changes are evolutionary. For example, the functionality, performance and architecture of a platform may change over a number of years. Each change brings with it an opportunity to provide better levels of service to the business. In evolutionary changes, it is possible to plan how to respond to the change and thus maintain stability while responding to the changes.

Many changes, though, happen very quickly and sometimes under extreme pressure. For example a Business Unit unexpectedly wins a contract that requires additional IT services, more capacity and faster response times. The ability to respond to this type of change without impacting other services is a significant challenge. Many IT organisations are unable to achieve this balance and tend to focus on either the stability of the IT Infrastructure or the ability to respond to changes quickly.

Achieving balance between quality of service and cost of service

Service Operation is required consistently to deliver the agreed level of IT service to its customers and users, while at the same time keeping costs and resource utilisation at an optimal level (Figure 8.3).

Figure 8.3 Achieving a balance between focus on cost and quality (Source: OGC ITIL Service Operation ISBN 978-0-113310-46-3)

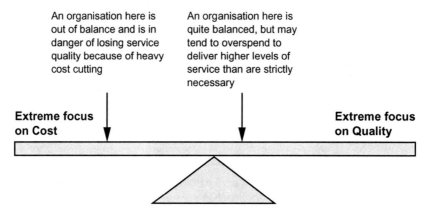

An organisation here is out of balance and is in danger of losing service quality because of heavy cost cutting

An organisation here is quite balanced, but may tend to overspend to deliver higher levels of service than are strictly necessary

Extreme focus on Cost

Extreme focus on Quality

Early in the life of a service it is possible to deliver significant improvement in service quality with relatively small amounts of money. However, later in a service's life, even small improvements in the quality of a service are very expensive.

It is possible to increase quality while reducing costs. This is normally instigated by Service Operation and progressed by CSI. Achieving an optimal balance between cost and quality is a key overall objective of Service Management. Achieving this balance will ensure delivery of the level of service necessary to meet business requirements at an optimal cost.

Achieving balance between being too reactive or too proactive

- A reactive organisation is one which does not act unless it is prompted to do so by an external driver.
- A proactive organisation is always looking for ways to improve the current situation.

An unfortunate reality in many organisations is that a focus on reactive management, mistakenly as the sole means, to ensure services are highly consistent and stable, actively discourages proactive behaviour from operational staff. The unfortunate irony of this approach is that discouraging effort investment in proactive Service Management can ultimately increase the effort and cost of reactive activities and further risk stability and consistency in services (Figure 8.4).

Figure 8.4 Achieving a balance between being too reactive or too proactive
[Source: OGC ITIL Service Operation ISBN 978-0-113310-46-3]

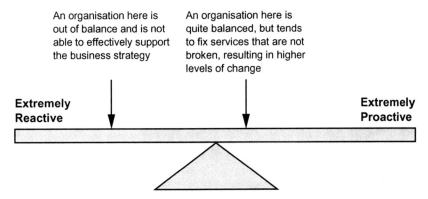

Proactive behaviour is usually seen as positive, especially since it enables the organisation to maintain competitive advantage in a changing environment. However, being too proactive can be expensive and can result in staff being distracted. The need for proper balance in reactive and proactive behaviour often achieves the optimal result.

Less mature service provider organisations tend to be more reactive, whereas more mature service providers tend to be more proactive because they have more data and information for forecasting and predicting.

SYLLABUS REFERENCE: ITILMD04-13

Understand and explain the conflicting balances in Service Operation.

Self-help

Many organisations find it beneficial to offer 'Self-help' capabilities to their users. The technology should therefore support this capability with some form of 24/7 web front-end offering an automated, menu-driven range of self-help and Service Requests with a direct interface into the back-end process-handling software.

This would enable users to resolve their own difficulties and might include, as appropriate:

- frequently asked questions (FAQs) and solutions;
- 'how to do' search capabilities to guide users through a context-sensitive list of tasks or activities;
- a bulletin-type service containing details of outstanding service issues/ problems together with anticipated restoration times;
- password change capabilities using secure password protection software to check identities, perform authorisation and change passwords without the need for Service Desk intervention;
- software fix downloads (patches, service packs, bug fixes etc. where it is determined that the user has the wrong version or a fix is needed) – tools are available to automate the checking process, to compare the actual desktop image with the agreed 'standard' builds and to allow upgrades to be offered and accepted where necessary;
- software repairs where it is detected that a corruption may have occurred, to allow software fixes, removal and/or reinstallation;
- software removal requests automatically completed with any licence being returned to the pool;
- downloads of additional software packages – tools are available to check a predefined software policy and to allow the download of additional software packages, if covered by the policy. This can include automated software licence checks and financial approvals as well as CMS updating;
- advanced notice of any planned downtime or service outages or degradations – the self-help solution should include the capability for users to log Incidents themselves, which can be used during periods that the Service Desk is closed and attended to by Service Desk staff at the start of the next shift.

Event types

> **EVENT**
>
> A change of state which has significance for the management of a configuration item or IT service.

An event can also be defined as any detectable or discernible occurrence that has significance for the management of the IT infrastructure or the delivery of IT services. The term event is also used to mean an alert or notification created by any service, Configuration Item or monitoring tool. Events typically require IT operations personnel to take actions, and often lead to Incidents being logged.

There are many different types of event, but each organisation should categorise events into at least three types, including:

- **Informational events:** events that do not require any action, that often signify normal operation. They are typically stored in the system in log or journal files and are often used to generate statistics. Examples include:

  - a user has logged on to an application;
  - a scheduled workload has completed;
  - a device has come online.

- **Warning events:** events that signify unusual, but not exceptional operation, normally generated when a service or device is approaching a threshold to notify the appropriate person, process or tool so that the situation can be checked and appropriate action taken. Warnings are not typically raised for device failures. Examples include:

  - a server's memory utilisation reaches within 5 per cent of its highest acceptable performance level;
  - the completion time for a transaction is 50 per cent longer than usual;
  - the error rate on the network has increased by 20 per cent in the last hour.

- **Exception events:** events usually raised for services or devices that are operating abnormally. Typically this means that an SLA or OLA has been breached and the business is being impacted. Exceptions could represent failure, impaired functionality or degraded performance. Examples include:

  - a server is down;
  - a user attempts to log on with an incorrect password;
  - a device's processor utilisation is above the acceptable level.

The type of event indicates the severity or significance of what has occurred.

ALERT

A warning that a threshold has been reached, something has changed or a failure has occurred.

Alerts are generally used to indicate that either a warning event or an exception event has occurred and action needs to be taken.

PROCESSES

The main Processes within the Service Operation stage of the Lifecycle are:

- Event Management;
- Incident Management*;
- Request Fulfilment;
- Problem Management*;
- Access Management.

There are also other operational activities of Processes covered in other Lifecycle phases that are performed by operational functions. These are described later within this section.

The two of these Processes identified with an asterisk were contained in ITIL v2 and only changes have been covered within this section. Changes were made within the Problem Management process. The other four areas are considered in more detail.

Event Management
Purpose, goal, objectives and scope
The purpose of Event Management activities is to provide the ability to detect events, make sense of them and determine the appropriate control action to be taken.

The objectives of Event Management include:

- to provide a basis for automating many routine Operations Management activities;
- to provide an entry point for many Service Operation activities;
- to provide a way of comparing actual performance and behaviour against design standards and SLAs.

The scope of the Event Management process should include any aspect of Service Management that needs to be controlled and which could be automated, including:

- Configuration Items (CIs);
- environmental conditions;
- software licence monitoring to ensure optimum legal licence utilisation and allocation;
- intrusion detection;
- normal activity, such as the performance of a server.

Event Management activities
Figure 8.5 shows a high-level and generic representation of an Event Management process.

Figure 8.5 The Event Management process (Source: OGC ITIL Service Operation
ISBN 978-0-113310-46-3)

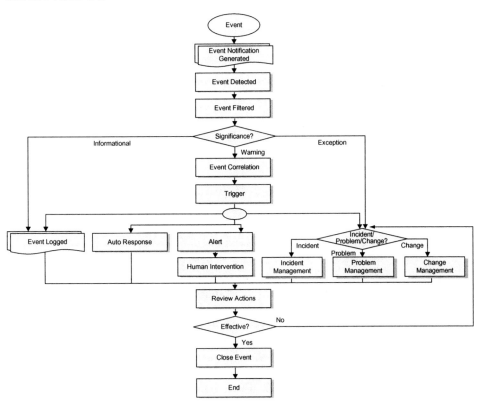

The key activities involved in the Event Management process are:

- **Event notification and detection:** when events occur within the
  infrastructure most CIs are designed to communicate the information in
  two ways:

  - A device is interrogated or polled by a management tool and information
    requested.

  - The CI generates a notification when certain conditions are met. Once an
    event has been notified it will be detected by an agent or management
    tool specifically designed to interpret the meaning of the event.

- **Event filtering:** the purpose of event filtering is to decide what type of
  event has occurred and whether further action is required. If the event is
  informational then it will normally be recorded and no further action taken.
  Filtering is the first level of correlation and is used to determine the
  significance of the event and to determine the course of action to process
  the event.

151

- **Event correlation:** if an event is significant, then a decision must be made as to what action is required. It is at this stage that the meaning of the event is determined. Correlation is normally performed by a 'Correlation Engine' within a management tool which compares events with a set of rules and criteria in order to determine the business impact of the event. Once this has been done an impact and priority can be associated with the event and a 'trigger' or 'alert' can be raised to initiate the required response.

- **Event response:** there are normally a number of alternative responses and each organisation should have its own range of responses, which should include:

  - **Event logged:** all events should be recorded. For information events that is all that is necessary, but for other types of events further action will probably be needed.

  - **Auto response:** some events are understood enough that an appropriate response can be defined and automated.

  - **Alert and human intervention:** if an event needs human intervention it will need to be escalated. The purpose of the alert is to ensure that a person or team with the right skills to process the event is notified.

  - **Incident, Problem or change:** some events are caused by a situation where the appropriate response will require to be handled through the Incident, Problem or Change Management process. Some events may require one or a combination of the following actions to be taken: open an RFC; open an Incident record; open or link to a Problem record.

  - **Special types of incident:** in some cases an event will indicate an event that does not directly impact any IT service, for instance a redundant network link fails. In this case a non-operational Incident should still be raised and referred to the appropriate team.

- **Review actions:** not all events can be reviewed, but it is important that significant events are reviewed and checked to ensure they have been handled appropriately. This review will normally provide input to the continual improvement of the Event Management process.

- **Close event:** most events are not opened and closed, but some events remain open or recur until certain action is taken. It is sometimes difficult to relate the open event to the corresponding close notification. With events that generate Incidents, Problems or changes these should be formally closed with a link to the appropriate records from other processes.

Process KPIs and challenges

Some of the main KPIs of the Event Management process that should be considered for measuring the effectiveness of the activities are:

- number of events by category;
- number of events by significance;

- number and percentage of events that required human intervention and whether this was performed;
- number and percentage of events that resulted in Incidents or changes;
- number and percentage of events caused by existing Problems or known errors;
- number and percentage of repeated or duplicated events;
- number and percentage of events indicating performance;
- number and percentage of events indicating potential availability issues (e.g. failovers to alternative devices or excessive workload swapping);
- number and percentage of each type of event per platform or application;
- number and ratio of events compared with the number of Incidents.

The challenges facing the Event Management process are:

- obtaining funding for the necessary tools and effort needed to install and exploit the benefits of the tools;
- setting the correct level of filtering – setting the level of filtering incorrectly can result in either being flooded with relatively insignificant events or not being able to detect relatively important events until it is too late;
- rolling out of the necessary monitoring agents across the entire IT infrastructure may be a difficult and time-consuming activity requiring an ongoing commitment over quite a long period of time;
- acquiring the necessary skills can be time-consuming and costly.

Request fulfilment

SERVICE REQUEST

A request from a user for information, or advice, or for a Standard change or for access to an IT service. For example to reset a password or to provide standard IT services for a new user. Service Requests are usually handled by a Service Desk and do not require an RFC to be submitted.

Purpose, goal, objectives and scope
The purpose of Request Fulfilment activities is to provide a process for handling Service Requests in a timely manner as a separate work stream.

The objectives of Request Fulfilment include:

- to provide a channel for users to request and receive standard services for which a predefined approval and qualification process exists;
- to provide information to users and customers about the availability of services and the procedure for obtaining them;

- to source and deliver the components of requested standard services (e.g. licences and software media);
- to assist with general information, complaints or comments.

The scope of the Request Fulfilment process should include the processing of all Service Requests. There is a significant difference between an Incident and a Service Request. An Incident is usually an unplanned event, whereas a Service Requests is usually something that can and should be planned.

Many Service Requests are actually small changes: low risk, frequently occurring and low cost. Their scale, frequency and low-risk nature means that they are better handled by a separate Process rather than being allowed to congest the normal Incident or Change Management processes. The ownership of Service Requests resides with the Service Desk.

The Request Fulfilment activities
The Request Fulfilment process should consist of the following activities:

- **Definition of request models:** many Service Requests will be frequently occurring and would be better handled using a predefined process flow within a model which could also include pre-approval, groups involved, targets and escalation paths.

- **Providing menu selection:** Request Fulfilment offers great opportunities for self-help facilities, using 'menu-type' selection using web interfaces so that users can select from predefined lists. This type of 'shopping basket' experience can then be linked directly to back-end tools and applications for the management of the Request Fulfilment activities.

- **Financial approval:** most requests will have some form of financial implication and therefore the cost of the request will need to be provided and submitted to the user for their approval.

- **Other approval:** in some cases further approval may be required, such as compliance-related or wider business approval.

- **Fulfilment:** the fulfilment activity will depend on the nature of the request. Some simpler requests may be completed by the Service Desk and others will have to be forwarded to specialist groups or suppliers for fulfilment.

- **Closure:** when the Service Request has been fulfilled it must be returned back to the Service Desk for closure.

Process KPIs and challenges
Some of the main KPIs of the Request Fulfilment process that should be considered for measuring the effectiveness of the activities are:

- the total number of Service Requests (as a control measure);
- breakdown of Service Requests at each stage (e.g. logged, work in progress (WIP), closed etc.);

- the size of current backlog of outstanding Service Requests;

- the mean elapsed time for handling each type of Service Request;

- the number and percentage of Service Requests completed within agreed target times;

- the average cost per type of Service Request;

- the level of client satisfaction with the handling of Service Requests (as measured in some form of satisfaction survey).

The challenges facing the Request Fulfilment process are:

- clearly defining and documenting the type of Requests that will be handled within the Request Fulfilment process (and those that will either go through the Service Desk and be handled as Incidents or those that will need to go through formal Change Management), so that all parties are absolutely clear on the scope;

- establishing self-help front-end capabilities that allow the users to interface successfully with the Request Fulfilment process.

Access Management
Purpose, goal, objectives and scope
The purpose of Access Management activities is to provide the right for users to be able to use a service or group of services. It is therefore the execution of policies and actions defined in Security and Availability Management.

The objectives of Access Management include:

- to provide access to services or groups of services for authorised users;

- to implement the policies and guidelines of Information Security and Availability Management.

The scope of the Access Management process is effectively the execution of Information Security and Availability Management policies, processes and guidelines. Access Management is the Process that enables users to use the services that are documented in the Service Catalogue. It enables the management of confidentiality, availability and integrity of the organisation's data and intellectual property.

The Access Management activities
Access Management is normally executed by Technical and Application Management functions and is not usually a separate function. Access Management can usually be initiated by a Service Request through the Service Desk.

Access Management uses the following terms:

- **Access:** refers to the level and extent of a service's functionality or data that a user is entitled to use.

- **Identity:** refers to the information about the user that distinguishes them as an individual and which verifies their status within the organisation. By definition, the identity of a user is unique to that user.

- **Rights:** (also called privileges) refer to the actual settings whereby a user is provided access to a service or group of services. Typical rights, or levels of access, include read, write, execute, change, delete.

- **Services or service groups:** most users do not use only one service, and users performing a similar set of activities will use a similar set of services. Instead of providing access to each service for each user separately, it is more efficient to be able to grant each user, or group of users, access to the whole set of services that they are entitled to use at the same time.

- **Directory Services:** refer to a specific type of tool that is used to manage access and rights.

The Access Management process should consist of the following activities:

- **Requesting access:** access or restriction can be requested by:

  - a standard request by the Human Resource system;

  - a Request for Change (RFC);

  - a Service Request submitted via the Request Fulfilment process;

  - execution of a pre-authorised script or option.

- **Verification:** each request for access needs to be verified to ensure that the user is who they say they are and they have a legitimate requirement to access the service. This will usually be achieved by the user providing their username and password in collaboration with some independent verification from Human Resources or Security.

- **Providing rights:** Access Management does not decide who has access to which services. Access Management executes the policies and regulations defined by Service Strategy and Service Design. As soon as a user has been verified, Access Management will provide the user with the rights to use the requested services.

- **Monitoring identity status:** users' roles change and so do their access needs for services. Access Management should document user lifecycles and use these to automate the process.

- **Logging and tracking access:** Access Management is also responsible for ensuring the access rights it has allocated are being properly used. Access monitoring and control should be included in the activities of all Technical and Application Management functions and all Service Management processes.

- **Removing or restricting rights:** Access Management is also responsible for removing or restricting access based on the decisions and policies of Service Strategy and Service Design.

Process KPIs and challenges

Some of the main KPIs of the Access Management process that should be considered for measuring the effectiveness of the activities are:

- number of requests for access (Service Request, RFC etc.);
- instances of access granted by service, user, department etc.;
- instances of access granted by department or individual granting rights;
- number of Incidents requiring a reset of access rights;
- number of Incidents caused by incorrect access settings.

The challenges facing the Access Management process are:

- the ability to verify the identity of users and authorisers;
- the ability to maintain accurate records of users, their access levels and changing requirements over time.

SYLLABUS REFERENCE: ITILMD05-5a

Explain the objectives, scope, concepts, activities, key metrics, roles and challenges for Event Management, Request Fulfilment and Access Management.

Operational activities (of Processes covered in other Lifecycle stages)

There are also several other activities that Service Operation should be performing based on the requirements of Processes within other stages of the Lifecycle for operational activities. These are activities completed in liaison with, and under the direction of, the actual Processes themselves and are summarised here.

Change Management

- Raising RFCs for Service Operation issues and using the Change Management process.
- Participating in CAB or Change Advisory Board/Emergency Committee (CAB/EC) meetings.
- Implementing or backing out changes within the scope of Service Operation, when required.
- Helping define and maintain Service Operation change models.
- Ensuring staff are made aware of change schedules.

Configuration Management

- Informing Configuration Management of any discrepancies found in the CMS;
- Making any amendments to Service Operation components and services.

Release and Deployment Management

- Implementation activities relating to Service Operation components and services for the deployment of new releases.
- Participating in the planning of new releases to advise on Service Operation issues.
- The physical handling of CIs from and to the DML as required.

Capacity Management

- Monitoring of infrastructure components.
- Working with technical support groups to assist with the resolution of performance-related Incidents and Problems.
- Assistance with the implementation of any required performance restrictions or limitations required by Demand Management.
- Assistance with any adjustments or rescheduling requirements of Workload Management.
- Assisting with the evaluation of the accuracy of modelling and trending predictions.
- Assisting with the production of the Capacity Plan.

Availability Management

- Assisting the design activities with the ongoing improvement of existing services and their design.
- Assisting with the review of maintenance activities, major Problem reviews and specific initiatives such as Service Failure Analysis or Component Failure Impact Analysis exercises.

Knowledge Management

- Assisting with the capture, storage of, and access to all Service Operation information and documentation.

Financial Management

- Assisting with the preparation and management of budgets and budget estimates.

IT Service Continuity Management

- Assisting with the testing and execution of systems and service continuity and recovery plans.
- All Service Operation functions must be on the Business Continuity Central coordination Team.
- Assistance with specific activities such as Risk Assessment and Management.

Problem Management changes

The areas of Problem Control and Error Control have been removed, but the activities are still included within the reactive activities of Problem Management. Also the raising of a Known Error Record has been changed as follows.

As soon as the diagnosis is complete, and particularly where a workaround has been found (even though it may not yet be a permanent resolution), a Known Error Record must be raised and placed in the Known Error Database, so that if further Incidents or Problems arise, they can be identified and the service restored more quickly. However, in some cases it may be advantageous to raise a Known Error Record even earlier in the overall process (e.g. simply for information purposes), even though the diagnosis may not be complete or a workaround found, so it is inadvisable to set a concrete procedural point exactly when a Known Error Record must be raised.

The Known Error Record should be raised as soon as it becomes useful to do so!

SYLLABUS REFERENCE: ITILMD13-4

Understand the changes made at ITIL v3 to Problem Management.

ROLES, RESPONSIBILITIES AND FUNCTIONS

A function is a logical concept that refers to the people and automated measures that execute a defined process, an activity or a combination of Processes or activities. The Service Operation functions are needed to manage the 'steady state' operational IT environment. This means that Technical and Application Management can be organised in any combination and number of departments. The second-level groupings in Figure 8.6 are examples of typical groups of activities performed by Technical Management and are not a suggested organisation structure.

Service Desk

Service Desk provides a central point of contact for all IT users and is responsible for providing the first point of contact and support. Service Desk should not be underrated and can often compensate for deficiencies elsewhere in the service provider organisation. The objective of the Service Desk is to restore 'normal service' to the users as soon as possible.

The Service Desk is normally responsible for recording Incidents and the management of Incidents throughout their lifecycle. It is also responsible for the initial handling and the closure of Service Requests ensuring that they are referred to the appropriate teams, departments or suppliers for their fulfilment.

Service Desk is typically not involved in Event Management unless an event requires some response that is within the Service Desk's defined activity. Generally event handling is performed by IT Operations staff or an Operations Bridge.

Figure 8.6 Service Operation functions (Source: OGC ITIL Service Operation ISBN 978-0-113310-46-3)

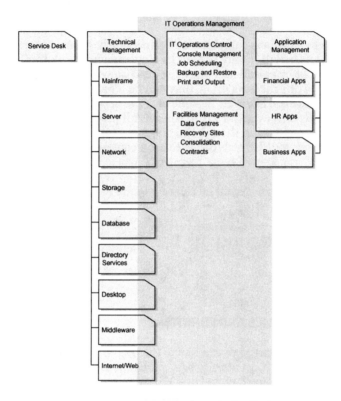

There are many types of Service Desk and each organisation needs to choose the most appropriate for their needs. The most common types of Service Desk are:

- a local Service Desk;
- a centralised Service Desk;
- a virtual Service Desk;
- a 'Follow the Sun' Service Desk.

These are similar to the Service Desk types described in ITIL v2.

IT Technical Management

Technical Management provides detailed technical skills and resources needed to support the ongoing operation of the IT infrastructure. Technical Management also plays an important role in the design, testing, release and improvement of IT services. Technical Management refers to the groups, departments and teams that provide technical expertise and overall management of the IT infrastructure.

Technical Management fulfils two roles:

- It is responsible for the technical knowledge and expertise relating to the management of the IT infrastructure. It ensures that the knowledge required to design, build, transition, operate and improve the technology is identified, developed and refined.

- It provides the resources required to support the ITSM Lifecycle. It ensures that the technical resources are effectively trained and deployed to design, build, transition, operate and improve the technology.

By performing these two roles, Technical Management ensures that the organisation has access to the right level of human resources to manage the technology and that there is the right balance between the skill level, utilisation and cost of these resources. This is especially true with regard to expensive specialist staff who need to be used on tactical, project and problem resolution activities.

The objectives of Technical Management are to assist, plan, implement and maintain a stable infrastructure supporting an organisation's business processes through:

- well-designed, highly resilient and cost-effective infrastructure topology;

- the use of technical skills to maintain the technical infrastructure in optimum condition;

- the use of technical skills to speedily diagnose and resolve any technical failures.

IT Operations Management

IT Operations Management is the function responsible for the daily operational activities needed to manage the IT infrastructure. This is done according to the Performance Standards defined during Service Design. IT Operations Management is the function responsible for the ongoing management and maintenance of an organisation's IT infrastructure to ensure delivery of the agreed level of service to the business.

IT Operations Management has two main roles:

- Responsibility for performing the activities and meeting the performance standards defined during Service Design and tested during Service Transition. Its primary role is to maintain a stable infrastructure and consistency of IT service.

- Responsibility for supporting the ability of the business to meet its objectives, which depend on the output and reliability of the day-to-day IT operations. IT Operations is part of the process of adding value to the business as a part of the overall value network.

IT operations must maintain a balance between these activities and roles, which will require the following:

- All staff to have an understanding of how technology and technology performance affect the delivery of IT services.

- An understanding of the relative importance and impact of the services.

- Processes, procedures and manuals.
- A clearly defined set of achievement metrics for reporting.
- A cost strategy for balancing the requirements of different Business Units with cost savings through the optimisation of technology.
- A value-based strategy for ROI rather than a cost-based one.

The objectives of IT Operations Management include:

- maintenance of the status quo to achieve stability of the organisation's day-to-day Processes and activities;
- regular monitoring and improvement to achieve higher quality service at reduced costs, while maintaining stability;
- rapid application of operational skills to diagnose and resolve IT operation failures.

Some Technical and Applications Management groups or teams will manage and execute their own operational activities, others will delegate these activities to a dedicated IT Operations function.

The main activities involved within IT Operations are:

- **Operations Control:** oversees the execution and management of the IT infrastructure operational events and activities. This can be accomplished using an Operations Bridge or Network Operations Centre. As well as performing routine tasks, Operations Control also performs specific tasks:

  - Console management: defining central observation and monitoring capability and using the consoles for monitoring and control activities.
  - Job scheduling: management of routine batch jobs, scripts and schedules.
  - Backup and restore: on behalf of all users, customers, teams and technology.
  - Print and output management: for the collation and distribution of all centralised printing and electronic output.
  - Maintenance activities: on behalf of all teams and departments.

- **Facilities Management:** manages the physical environments, data centre, computer rooms and recovery sites, including all power and cooling equipment.

Applications Management

Application Management is responsible for managing applications throughout their lifecycle (Figure 8.7).

This diagram clearly shows that within the Application Management lifecycle both Application Development and Application Management are involved in all stages. However, some of the stages are driven by Application Development with input from Application Management and in others Application Management will be driving the stage activities with input and support from Application Development.

Figure 8.7 Role of teams within the Application Management lifecycle (Source: OGC ITIL Service Operation ISBN 978-0-113310-46-3)

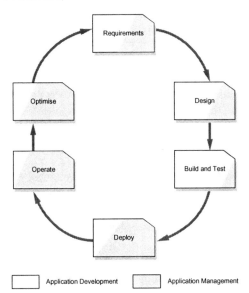

The Application Management function supports and maintains operational applications and also plays an important role in the design, testing and improvement of applications that form part of IT services.

Application Management is to applications what Technical Management is to the IT infrastructure. Application Management plays a role in all applications, whether purchased or developed in-house. One of the key decisions that they contribute to is whether to buy an application or build it.

Once that decision is made, Application Management will play a dual role:

- The custodian of technical knowledge and expertise related to managing applications. Application Management ensures that the knowledge required to design, test, manage and improve IT services is identified, developed and refined.
- Provision of the actual resources to support the ITSM Lifecycle. Application Management ensures that resources are effectively trained and deployed to design, build, transition, operate and improve the technology required to deliver and support IT services.

By performing these two roles, Application Management is able to ensure that the organisation has access to the right type and level of human resources to manage applications and thus to meet business objectives. Application Management is also responsible for maintaining a balance between the skill level and the cost of these resources.

In additional to these two high-level roles, Application Management also performs the following two specific roles:

- Providing guidance to IT Operations about how best to carry out the ongoing operational management of applications. This role is partly carried out during the Service Design process, but it is also a part of everyday communication with IT Operations Management as they seek to achieve stability and optimum performance.
- The integration of the Application Management lifecycle into the ITSM Lifecycle. This is discussed below along with the objectives, activities and structures that enable Application Management to play these roles effectively.

The objectives of Application Management are:

- support the organisation's business processes by helping to identify functional and manageability requirements for application software;
- to assist in the design and deployment of applications and the ongoing support and improvement of those applications.

These objectives are achieved through:

- applications that are well designed, resilient and cost-effective;
- ensuring that the required functionality is available to achieve the required business outcomes;
- the organisation of adequate technical skills to maintain operational applications in optimum condition;
- the swift use of technical skills to rapidly diagnose and resolve any technical failures that do occur.

One of the key decisions in Application Management is whether to buy an application that supports the required functionality or whether to build the application specifically for the organisation's requirements. These decisions are often made by a Chief Technical Officer (CTO) or Steering Committee, but they are dependent on information from a number of sources. These are discussed in detail in Service Design, but are summarised here from an Application Management function perspective. Application Management will assist in this decision during the service.

SYLLABUS REFERENCE: ITILMD06

Explain the role, objective, organisational structures, staffing and metrics of the Service Operation functions.

Organising for Service Operation

Each service provider organisation will have to make its own decision on the structure of the functions within Service Operation. Some different options are discussed below.

Organisation by technical specialisation

In this type of organisation, departments and teams are created according to technology and the skills and activities needed to manage that technology. This structure as shown in Figure 8.8 can work well provided that these groups are fully represented in the Service Design, Transition and Improvement processes.

Figure 8.8 IT Operations organised according to technical specialisation (example)
(Source: OGC ITIL Service Operation ISBN 978-0-113310-46-3)

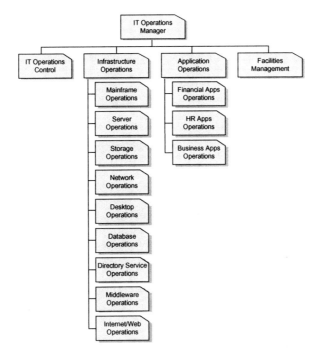

The advantages and disadvantages this organisational structure are summarised in Table 8.1.

Organisation by activity

This type of organisation, shown in Figure 8.9, is based on the fact that similar activities have to be performed on all technologies. This means that people who perform similar activities, regardless of technology, are grouped together, although within each department there may be teams focusing on specific areas of technology. In this type of organisation there is no clear differentiation between the different Technical and Application Management areas.

The advantages and disadvantages of this organisational structure are summarised in Table 8.2.

Table 8.1 Advantages and disadvantages of organisation by technical specialisation

Advantages of this structure	Disadvantages of this structure
It is easier to set internal performance objectives since all staff in a single department have a similar set of tasks on a similar technology.	When people are divided into separate departments the priorities of their own group tend to override the priorities of other departments.
Individual devices, systems or platforms can be managed more effectively since people with the appropriate skills are dedicated to manage these and measured according to their performance.	Knowledge about the infrastructure and relationships between components is difficult to collect and fragmented. Each group collects and keeps their own information.
Managing training programmes is easier since skill sets are clearly defined and separated into specific groups.	Each technology managed by a group is seen as a separate entity. This becomes a problem on systems that consist of components managed by different teams.
	It is more difficult to understand the impact of a single department's poor performance on the IT service.
	It is more difficult to track overall IT service performance since each group is being measured on an individual basis.
	Coordinating Change Assessments and Schedules is more difficult since many different departments have to provide input for each change.

(Continued)

Table 8.1 *(Continued)*

Advantages of this structure	Disadvantages of this structure
	Work requiring knowledge of multiple technologies is difficult since most resources are only trained for and concerned with the management of a single technology. Projects therefore have to include cross-training, which is expensive.

Organisation to manage Processes

In process-based organisations people are organised into groups or departments that perform or manage a specific Process. This is similar to the activity-based structure except that departments focus on end-to-end sets of activities rather than on one individual activity.

It is generally not a good idea to structure the whole organisation around Processes. Processes are used to overcome the 'silo' effect, not to actually create 'silos'. However, there are a number of Processes that will probably need a dedicated organisational structure to support and manage them.

The advantages and disadvantages of this organisational structure are summarised in Table 8.3.

Organisation by geography

IT Operations can be physically distributed and, in some cases, each location needs to be organised according to its own particular context. This structure (Figure 8.10) is often used where data centres and technologies are geographically distributed and there are different business models, cultures and regulations in different countries or regions.

The advantages and disadvantages of this organisational structure are summarised in Table 8.4.

Hybrid organisation structures

It is unlikely that IT Operations will be structured using only one type of organisational structure. Most organisations use a technical specialisation with

Figure 8.9 A department based on executing a set of activities (Source: OGC ITIL Service Operation ISBN 978-0-113310-46-3)

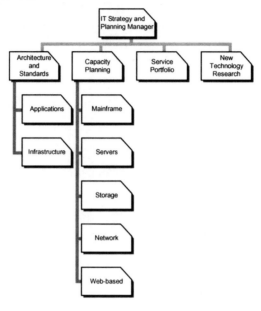

Table 8.2 Advantages and disadvantages of organisation by activity

Advantages of this structure	Disadvantages of this structure
It is easier to manage groups of related activities since all the people involved in these activities report to the same manager.	Resources with similar skills may be duplicated across different functions, which results in higher costs.
Measurement of teams or departments is based more on output than on isolated activities. This helps to build higher levels of assurance that a service can be delivered.	Although measurement is more output-based, it is still focused on the performance of internal activities rather than driven by the experience of the customer or end-user.

Table 8.3 Advantages and disadvantages of organisation to manage Processes

Advantages of this structure	Disadvantages of this structure
Processes are easier to define.	A basic principle of Processes is that they are a means of linking the activities of various departments and groups. By using Processes as a basis for organisational design, additional Processes need to be defined to ensure that the departments work together.
There is less role conflict as job descriptions and process role descriptions are the same. In other structures a single job description will typically include activities for several roles.	Even if a department is responsible for executing a Process, there will still be external dependencies. Groups may not view Process activities outside of their own Process as being important, resulting in Processes that cannot be fully executed because dependencies cannot be met.
Metrics of team or department performance and process performance are the same, effectively aligning 'internal' and 'external' metrics.	While some aspects of a Process can be centralised, there will always be a number of activities that will have to be performed by other groups. The relationship between the dedicated team or department and the people performing the decentralised activities is often difficult to define and manage.

Figure 8.10 IT Operations organised according to geography (Source: OGC ITIL Service Operation ISBN 978-0-113310-46-3)

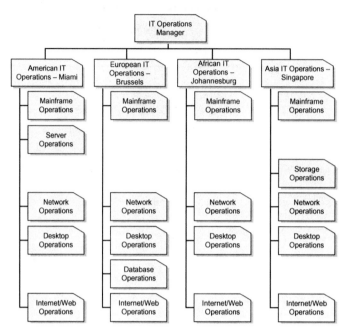

some activity-, process- or geography-based departments. The type of structure used and the exact combination of structures and departments will depend on the needs of organisation.

Combined Technical and Applications Management organisation structures
One last type of organisational structure should be considered. This structure incorporates IT Operations, Technical and Application Managements departments into a single structure. This is sometimes used where all of the groups are located within a single data centre. In this case the Data Centre Manager could take responsibility for all areas as shown in Figure 8.11.

The advantages and disadvantages of this organisational structure are summarised in Table 8.5.

Table 8.4 Advantages and disadvantages of organisation by geography

Advantages of this structure	Disadvantages of this structure
Organisation structure can be customised to meet local conditions.	Reporting lines and authority structures can be confusing. For example, does Network Operations report into the local Data Centre Manager or to a centralised Network Operations Manager?
IT Operations can be customised to meet differing levels of IT service from region to region.	Operational standards are difficult to impose, resulting in inconsistent and duplicated activities and tools, which increases the overall cost of operations.
	Duplication of roles, activities, tools and facilities across multiple locations could be very costly.
	Shared services, such as email, are more difficult to deliver as each regional organisation operates differently.
	Communication with customers and inside IT will be more difficult as they are not co-located and it may be difficult for staff in one location to understand the priorities of customers or staff in another location.

Figure 8.11 Centralised IT Operations Technical and Application Management structure (Source: OGC ITIL Service Operation ISBN 978-0-113310-46-3)

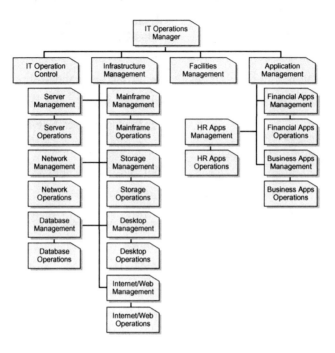

Table 8.5 Advantages and disadvantages of organisation by combined Technical and Applications Management

Advantages of this structure	Disadvantages of this structure
Organisation structure can be customised to meet local conditions.	Reporting lines and authority structures can be confusing.
Technical and Application Management can be customised to meet differing levels of IT service from region to region.	Standards are difficult to impose, resulting in inconsistent and duplicated activities and tools, resulting in reduced economies of scale, which in turn increases the overall cost of operations

(Continued)

Table 8.5 *(Continued)*

Advantages of this structure	Disadvantages of this structure
	Duplication of roles, activities, tools and facilities across multiple locations could be very costly.

SYLLABUS REFERENCE: ITILMD07-3

Understand the organisational issues surrounding the Service Operation organisational structures.

9　CONTINUAL SERVICE IMPROVEMENT

LEARNING OBJECTIVES

The purpose of this chapter is to help candidates understand all the aspects of the Continual Service Improvement (CSI) stage of the Lifecycle, including:

- the purpose, goals, objectives and value;
- the key concepts, definitions, principles and models;
- the Processes;
- the roles, responsibilities and functions.

PURPOSE, GOALS, OBJECTIVES AND VALUE

The primary purpose of CSI is to continually align and realign IT services to changing business needs by identifying and implementing improvements to IT services that support business Processes. These improvement activities support the Lifecycle approach through Service Strategy, Service Design, Service Transition and Service Operation. In effect, CSI is about looking for ways to improve Process effectiveness and efficiency, as well as cost-effectiveness.

If Service Management processes are not implemented, managed and supported using clearly defined goals, objectives and relevant measurements that lead to actionable improvements, the business will suffer. Depending on the criticality of a specific IT service to the business, the organisation could lose productive hours, experience higher costs, loss of reputation or, perhaps, even a business failure. That is why it is critically important to understand what to measure, why it is being measured and carefully define the successful outcome.

The main objectives of CSI are:

- to review, analyse and make recommendations on improvement opportunities in each Lifecycle phase: Service Strategy, Service Design, Service Transition and Service Operation;
- to review and analyse Service Level Achievement results;

- to identify and implement individual activities to improve IT service quality and improve the efficiency and effectiveness of enabling ITSM processes;
- to improve cost-effectiveness of delivering IT services without sacrificing customer satisfaction;
- to ensure applicable quality management methods are used to support continual improvement activities.

The scope of CSI needs to include the three main areas of:

- the overall health of Service Management as a discipline;
- the continual alignment of the Service Portfolio with current and future business needs;
- the maturity of the enabling Processes for each service in the continual Service Lifecycle model.

SYLLABUS REFERENCE: ITILMD02-10

Understand and explain the main goals and objectives of Continual Service Improvement.

The value of CSI to the business is delivered in four main ways:

- **Improvements:** outcomes that, when compared with the 'before state', show an increase in a desirable metric or a decrease in an undesirable metric.
- **Benefits:** the gains achieved through the realisation of improvements, often expressed in financial terms, although often benefits can be intangible, such as increased brand image or customer satisfaction.
- **Return on Investment (ROI):** the difference between the benefit (saving) and the amount expended (cost) to realise that benefit.
- **Value on Investment (VOI):** the extra value created by establishing benefits that include non-monetary or long-term outcomes. ROI is a sub-component of VOI.

SYLLABUS REFERENCE: ITILMD02-11

Fully comprehend and communicate what value Continual Service Improvement provides to the business.

KEY CONCEPTS, DEFINITIONS, PRINCIPLES AND MODELS

The key principles described within this section are:

- the CSI approach;
- the role of measurement;
- The Plan → Do → Check → Act (PDCA) model.

The CSI approach
The CSI approach is based on a continual cycle of improvement, itself based on the six steps shown in Figure 9.1.

Figure 9.1 The Continual Service Improvement (CSI) model (Source: OGC ITIL Continual Service Improvement ISBN 978-0-113310-49-4)

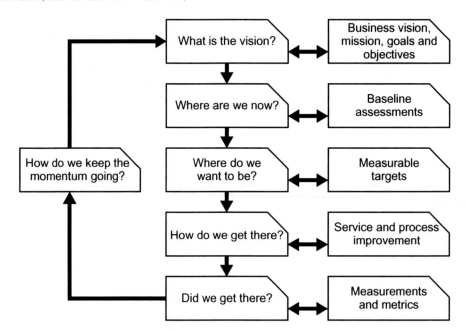

The six steps can be summarised as follows:

- Embrace the vision by understanding the high-level business objectives. The vision should align the business and IT strategies.
- Assess the current situation to obtain an accurate, unbiased snapshot of where the organisation is currently. This baseline assessment is an analysis of the current position in terms of the business, organisation, people, Processes and technology.

- Understand and agree on the priorities for improvement based on a deeper development of the principles defined in the vision. The full vision may be years away, but this step provides specific goals and a manageable time frame.

- Detail the CSI plan to achieve higher quality service provision by implementing ITSM processes.

- Verify that measurements and metrics are in place to ensure that milestones were achieved, Process compliance is high, and business objectives and priorities were met by the level of service.

- Finally, the Process should ensure that the momentum for quality improvement is maintained by assuring that changes become embedded in the organisation.

Reporting and communication are key activities within the use of this model and should be used to manage customer expectation and manage the gap between what the customer expects and what the service provider can deliver.

SYLLABUS REFERENCE: ITILMD04-14

Understand and explain the Continual Service Improvement model.

The role of measurement

Measurements and metrics are a key element of effective CSI activities. There are three types of metric that an organisation will need to collect to support CSI activities:

- **Technology metrics:** these metrics are often associated with component- and application-based metrics such as performance and availability.

- **Process metrics:** in the form of CSFs, KPIs and activity metrics from the Service Management processes, help determine the overall health of a Process. The four key areas of quality, performance, value and compliance help CSI in the identification of opportunities for improvement.

- **Service metrics:** are the result of measuring end-to-end service characteristics, often obtained from analysing component metrics.

Metrics are used in many business models including the Capability Maturity Model (CMM). Measurements and metrics can be used to track trends, productivity, resources and many other characteristics. Processes and groups are set goals and objectives to achieve. It is therefore important that organisations find some way of measuring performance by applying a set of measurements and metrics to each goal or objective.

Opinions of the number of CSFs and KPIs to use vary considerably. Some recommend that no more than two or three CSFs and KPIs should be used at any point in time for any one Process or service. Others recommend at least four or five should be used. This may not sound much, but when considering a number of services and a number of Processes, or when using a Balanced Scorecard approach the total number can be staggering.

It is recommended that in the early stages only a few CSFs and KPIs are defined, monitored and reported on, but as the maturity of the Processes and the organisation increases that more should be considered.

The delivery of products or services is a balanced trade-off between three elements:

- resources: the people and money (costs);
- features: the product or service and its quality (quality);
- schedules: the timescales (time).

Tension metrics can be used help create a balance by preventing teams or groups from focusing on just one element.

Business value
There are four reasons for monitoring and measuring:

- To validate previous decisions.
- To set direction for activities in order to meet set targets. It is the most prevalent reason for monitoring and measuring.
- To justify with factual evidence or proof, that a course of action is required.
- To identify a point of intervention including subsequent changes and corrective actions.

These actions ensure that measurements are designed to ensure that all activities, wherever possible, deliver increased value to the business.

These reasons for monitoring and measuring lead to three key questions:

- Why are we monitoring?
- When do we stop?
- Is there anyone using the data?

Too often organisations continue to measure long after the need has passed. Every time a report is produced the question 'Do we still need this?' should be asked. If the answer is 'No', then that reporting activity should be stopped.

Baselines
An important beginning to improvement activities is to establish baselines as starting points for later reference and comparison. Baselines are also useful in establishing an initial benchmark to determine if a service or Process needs to be improved. Baselines must be established at each level:

- strategic: goals and objectives;
- tactical: process maturity;
- operational: metrics and KPIs.

If a baseline is not established, then the first measurements will become the baseline.

SYLLABUS REFERENCE: ITILMD04-15

Understand the role of measurement for Continual Service Improvement and explain business value, baselines and types of metric.

The Plan → Do → Check → Act model

W. Edwards Deming proposed an approach to quality and its improvement based around four stages consisting of Plan, Do, Check, Act, sometimes referred to as the PDCA Model (Figure 9.2). After each cycle a consolidation activity should be undertaken and a baseline taken to prevent any regression, before initiating further improvement:

N.B.

Figure 9.2 The Deming Cycle (Source: OGC ITIL Continual Service Improvement ISBN 978-0-113310-49-4)

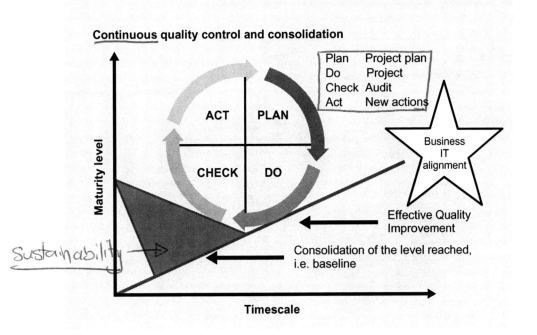

PROCESSES

The Seven-step Improvement Process
The main Process within the CSI stage of the Lifecycle is the Seven-step Improvement Process.

Purpose, goal, objectives and scope
The purpose of the Seven-step Improvement Process activities is to provide the ability to detect events, make sense of them and determine the appropriate control action is taken.

The objective of the Seven-step Improvement Process is to successfully implement improvements that deliver their predicted increase in business value.

The scope of the Seven-step Improvement Process should include any aspect of Service Management improvement that has been proposed for implementation within the organisation.

The Seven-step Improvement Process activities
The Seven-step Improvement Process is shown in Figure 9.3.

Figure 9.3 The Seven-step Improvement Process (Source: OGC ITIL Continual Service Improvement ISBN 978-0-113310-49-4)

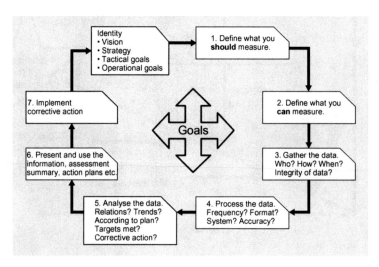

The key activities revolve around the seven steps of the process and the initial preceding activities required to direct the improvement actions:

- The **initial activities** should develop the vision, strategy, tactical goals and operational goals in line with Service Strategy. All of the goals should then be linked to objectives developed using the SMART (Specific-Measurable-Achievable-Relevant-Timely) principle.

- **Step 1 Define what you should measure:** Service Strategy and Service Design should have identified this information at the start of the Service Lifecycle. CSI can then start its cycle all over again at 'Where are we now?' This identifies the ideal situation for both the business and IT.

- **Step 2 Define what you can measure:** this activity is related to the CSI activities of 'Where do we want to be?' By identifying the new service level requirements of the business, the IT capabilities and the available budgets, CSI can conduct a gap analysis to identify the opportunities for improvements as well as answering the question 'How will we get there?'

- **Step 3 Gather the data:** in order to answer the 'Did we get there?' question, data must first be gathered based on the agreed goals and objectives. At this point the data is raw and no conclusions can be drawn.

- **Step 4 Process the data:** the data is processed in line with the agreed CSFs and KPIs. This means that time frames are coordinated, unaligned data is rationalised and made consistent and gaps in data are identified. The simple goal of this step is to process data from different sources into consistent and comparable data. Once the data has been rationalised analysis can begin.

- **Step 5 Analyse the data:** as the data is processed into information, it is analysed to identify service gaps, trends and the impact on the business. It is the analysing step that is most often overlooked or forgotten in the rush to present data to management.

- **Step 6 Present and use the information:** here the answer to 'Did we get there?' is formatted and communicated to present the various stakeholders with an accurate picture of the results of the improvement activities. Knowledge is presented to the business in a form that reflects their needs and assists them in determining the next steps.

- **Step 7 Implement corrective action:** the knowledge gained is used to optimise, improve and correct the service. Managers identify issues and present solutions. The corrective actions that need to be taken to improve the services are communicated and explained to the stakeholders. Following this step a new baseline is established and the cycle begins again.

The CSI processes should also include the following activities:

- Reviewing management information and trends to ensure that services are meeting agreed service levels.

- Reviewing management information and trends to ensure that the output of the enabling ITSM processes are achieving the desired results.

- Periodically conducting maturity assessments against the process activities and roles associated with the process activities to demonstrate areas of improvement or, conversely, areas of concern.
- Periodically conducting internal audits verifying employee and Process compliance.
- Reviewing existing deliverables for relevance.
- Making ad hoc recommendations for approval.
- Conducting periodic customer satisfaction surveys.
- Conducting external and internal service reviews to identify CSI opportunities.

Process KPIs and challenges

Some of the main KPIs of the Seven-step Improvement Process that should be considered for measuring the effectiveness of the activities are:

- number of improvement actions identified;
- percentage of improvements implemented on time and to budget;
- percentage of improvement actions successfully implemented.

Some of the major challenges facing the Seven-step Improvement Process are:

- a lack of management commitment;
- inadequate resources, budget and time;
- a lack of mature Service Management processes;
- a lack of information, monitoring and measurements;
- a lack of Knowledge Management;
- a resistance to planning and a reluctance to be proved wrong;
- a lack of corporate objectives, strategies, policies and business direction;
- a lack of IT objectives, strategies and policies;
- a lack of knowledge and appreciation of business impacts and priorities;
- diverse and disparate technologies and applications;
- resistance to change and cultural change;
- poor relationships, communication and a lack of cooperation between IT and the business;
- a lack of tools, standards and skills;
- tools too complex and costly to implement and maintain;
- over-commitment of resources with an associated inability to deliver (e.g. projects always late or over budget);
- poor supplier management and/or poor supplier performance.

ROLES, RESPONSIBILITIES AND FUNCTIONS

Roles
The roles described within the CSI activities are:

- Service Manager;
- CSI Manager;
- Service Owner;
- Process Owner;
- Knowledge Management;
- Reporting Analyst.

Service Manager, Service Owner and Process Owner are generic roles and have already been discussed previously in the section on generic roles in Chapter 4.

CSI Manager
The CSI Manager is ultimately responsible for the success of all improvements. The main responsibilities of the role are:

- responsibility for development of the CSI domain and for communicating the vision of CSI across the IT organisation;
- working with the Service Owner to identify and prioritise improvement opportunities;
- working with the Service Level Manager to identity service improvement plans and ensure that monitoring requirements are defined;
- ensuring that monitoring tools are in place to gather data;
- ensuring that baseline data is captured to measure improvement against it;
- defining and reporting on CSI CSFs, KPIs and CSI activity metrics;
- identifying other frameworks, models and standards that will support CSI activities;
- ensuring that Knowledge Management is an integral part of the day-to-day operations;
- ensuring that CSI activities are coordinated throughout the Service Lifecycle;
- reviewing analysed data;
- presenting recommendations to senior management for improvement;
- identifying, leading, managing and delivering cross-functional improvement projects;
- building effective relationships with the business and IT senior managers;
- setting direction and providing framework through which improvement objectives can be delivered;

- coaching, mentoring and supporting fellow service improvement professionals;
- possessing the ability to positively influence all levels of management to ensure that service improvement activities are receiving the necessary support.

Knowledge Management

Knowledge requires effective ownership within an organisation. The roles of knowledge and Knowledge Management ownership are vital to the success of knowledge sharing within an organisation. The key activities of this role include:

- ensuring compliance with organisational policies and processes;
- knowledge identification, capture and maintenance architectures;
- identifying, controlling and storing of information and knowledge;
- maintaining accurate information and knowledge;
- ensuring that information and knowledge are available to those that need it;
- publicising knowledge management systems and techniques;
- advising the business on Knowledge Management.

Reporting Analyst

The Reporting Analyst is a key role for CSI and often works with Service Level Management. They review and analyse data for component systems in order to obtain end-to-end service achievements and to identify trends. The main responsibilities are:

- participating in CSI meetings and SLM meetings to ensure the validity of the reporting metrics, notification thresholds and overall solution;
- responsibility for consolidating data from multiple sources;
- responsibility for producing trends and providing feedback on the trends, such as whether the trends are positive or negative, what their impact is likely to be and if the trends are predictable for the future;
- responsibility for producing reports on service or system performance based on the negotiated OLAs and SLAs and improvement initiatives.

SYLLABUS REFERENCE: ITILMD05-6

Explain the high level objectives, basic concepts, process activities, roles and metrics for the Seven-step Improvement Process.

10 TECHNOLOGY AND ARCHITECTURE

LEARNING OBJECTIVES

The purpose of this chapter is to help candidates:

- to understand and communicate how Service Automation helps integration of Service Management processes;
- to plan and implement Service Management technologies;
- to understand and weigh the generic requirements for an integrated set of Service Management Technology.

SERVICE AUTOMATION

The use of automation can have a significant impact on the performance of service assets such as management, organisation, people, Processes, knowledge and information. Advances in artificial intelligence, machine learning and rich media technologies have increased the capabilities of management tools and agents to handle a variety of tasks. Automation is considered to improve the Utility and Warranty of services and offers many advantages and opportunities including:

- the capacity of resources can be adjusted more easily in response to variations in demand;
- the provision of a good basis for measuring and improving services and Processes;
- easing many scheduling, routing and allocation problems and tasks that require calculating capability beyond the capacity of humans;
- the provision of a means of capturing knowledge required for services and Processes.

When appropriately applied, automation of Processes helps improve the quality of service, reduce costs and reduce risks, by reducing complexity and uncertainty and by efficiently resolving trade-offs. The areas where Service Management can benefit from automation include:

- design and modelling;
- the Service Catalogue;

- pattern recognition and analysis;
- classification, prioritisation and routing;
- detection and monitoring;
- optimisation.

It is also possible to handle routine tasks such as Service Requests with a level of automation. Such requests can be identified, classified and routed to automated services or self-service options.

Preparing for automation
Applying automation indiscriminately can create more problems or exacerbate existing ones. The following points need to be considered:

- Simplify the service processes before automating them, without affecting the Process outcomes.
- Clarify the flow of activities, allocation of tasks, need for information and interactions, so that all involved understand what they need to do.
- In self-service situations, reduce the surface area of contact that users have with the underlying systems and Processes to simplify the interface for the users.
- Do not be in a hurry to automate tasks and interactions that are neither simple nor routine. Recurring patterns are more suited to automation than less consistent and infrequent activities.

Service Analytics and instrumentation
Information is necessary for answering questions, but information is static. It only becomes knowledge when placed in the context of patterns and their implications. Those patterns give a high level of predictability and reliability about how the data will change over time. By understanding the patterns of information we can answer questions and predict future events and outcomes. This is Service Analytics and involves analysis to produce knowledge and synthesis to produce understanding. This is called the Data → Information → Knowledge → Wisdom (DIKW) hierarchy explained previously.

Although data does not answer any questions, it is a vital resource. Most organisations consider this capability in the form of instrumentation. The term instrumentation describes the technologies and techniques for measuring the behaviour of infrastructure elements. While data from element instrumentation is absolutely vital it is insufficient for monitoring services. A service's behaviour derives from the aggregate behaviour of its supporting elements. Information is the understanding of the relationships between pieces of data. Information answers four questions: Who? What? When? Where?

Service Analytics is useful for modelling existing infrastructure components and support services to the higher-level business services. This model is built on dependencies rather than topology. Infrastructure events are then tied to corresponding business processes. The component-to-system-to-process-linkage (also known as the service model) allows us to clearly identify the business impact of an event. Instead of responding to discrete events managers can characterise the behaviour of a service. This behaviour is then compared with a baseline of the normal behaviour for that time of day or business cycle.

This is as far along the DIKW hierarchy modern technologies allow. It is well understood that computer-based technology cannot provide wisdom. It requires people to provide evaluated understanding and answer the 'Why?' questions.

SYLLABUS REFERENCE: ITILMD08-2

Understand and communicate how service automation assists with integrating Service Management processes.

PLANNING AND IMPLEMENTING SERVICE MANAGEMENT TECHNOLOGIES

There are a number of factors that organisations need to plan for in readiness and during deployment and implementation of Service Management support tools. These include the following:

- licences;
- deployment;
- capacity checks;
- type of introduction.

Licences

The overall cost of Service Management tools, particularly integrated tools that form the heart of an integrated toolset, is usually determined by the number and type of user licence that the organisation needs. Such tools are often sold in modular format so the functionality of the modules and the number of users of each module will need to be well understood.

Licences are available in many different ways and vary depending on the supplier, but include:

- **dedicated licences:** required by staff that require frequent and prolonged access;
- **shared licences:** for staff that require less frequent access;
- **web licences:** useful for staff requiring remote access, generally with less functionality;
- **service on demand:** where access is provided by suppliers 'on demand' during periods of high demand. A variation of this is where the supplier offers it on a basis of Software as a Service (SaaS).

Deployment

Many Service Management tools require client/agent software deploying to target locations. This will need careful planning and should be handled though the Release and Deployment process.

Care needs to be taken to ensure that the Service Management tools are deployed at the appropriate time in relation to the organisation's level of capability and maturity.

A tool alone is not enough to make things work better. There is an old adage: 'A fool with a tool is still a fool!'

The organisation must first establish a 'service culture' and design the processes that the tool is seeking to address. It should also ensure that the staff are committed and understand the process and the way of working before deploying the tool.

Capacity checks

Some Capacity Management checks may be necessary before deploying agent software to ensure that there is sufficient storage and processing capability to host and run the new software. The capacity of the network will also need to be checked to ensure that it is capable of transferring all of the required management information.

Type of introduction

A decision is needed on what type of introduction is required: whether to go for a 'big bang' or a 'phased' approach. As most organisations will not start from a 'green field' situation and will have live services running during the introduction, a phased approach is more likely.

SYLLABUS REFERENCE: ITILMD08-3

Planning and implementing Service Management technologies.

GENERIC REQUIREMENTS

An integrated Service Management tool (or toolset) is needed to automate effective processes. Some organisations use an integrated set from a single supplier whereas other organisations prefer to integrate a number of tools from different suppliers. The set of tools should include the following core functionality:

- **Self-help:** the technology should support a self-help capability with a web front-end allowing web pages to be defined offering a menu-driven range of Self-help and Service Request facilities with a direct interface to back-end processing software.

- **Workflow or process engines:** a workflow or process control engine is needed to allow the pre-definition and control of defined processes such as the Request Fulfilment lifecycle, Change Models etc. This allows responsibilities, activities, timescales, escalation paths and alerting to be predefined and automatically managed.

- **Integrated CMS:** the tool should have an integrated CMS to allow the organisation's infrastructure assets, components, services and ancillary CIs (such as contracts, suppliers etc.) to be held together with all relevant attributes in a centralised location, allowing relationships between each to be stored and maintained.

- **Discovery/Deployment/Licensing technology:** in order to populate or verify CMS data and assist with licence management, discovery or automated audit tools will be required. These tools should be capable of being run from any location and allow interrogation and extraction of information relating to all components that make up or are connect to the IT infrastructure.

- **Remote Control:** the ability for Service Desk Analysts and other support groups to be able to take control of a user's desktop (under controlled security conditions) can assist the speedy resolution of issues.

- **Diagnostic scripts and utilities:** these help Service Desk analysts and support groups with early diagnosis of Incidents.

- **Reporting:** the technology should incorporate good reporting capability, as well as supporting standard interfaces which can be used to input data to industry standard reporting packages, dashboards etc.

- **Dashboards:** dashboard-type technology gives 'see at a glance' visibility of overall IT service performance and availability levels. Such displays can be included in management-style reports to users and customers and can also give real-time information for inclusion in web pages to give dynamic reporting, which can also help support diagnostic activities.

- **Integration with Business Service Management:** this supports the integration of Service Management applications, tools and information with business applications, tools and information, thereby giving closer business alignment and focus of all Service Management activities.

SERVICE DESIGN TOOLS

There are many tools and techniques that can be used to help with the design of services and their associated components. These enable:

- hardware design;
- software design;
- environmental design;
- Process design;
- data design.

These design tools help:

- to speed up the design process;
- to ensure that standards and conventions are followed;
- to support prototyping, modelling and simulation facilities;
- to enable 'What if ...?' scenarios;
- to enable interfaces and dependencies to be checked and correlated;
- to validate designs before they are developed and implemented.

Developing service designs can be simplified by the use of tools that provide graphical views of services and their constituent components, from the business process, through the service and the SLA, to the infrastructure, environment, data, applications, processes, OLAs, teams, contracts and suppliers. These tools can also provide 'drill-down' facilities to provide detailed information about components and, if linked to some form of 'metrics tree', can provide facilities to manage services through their lifecycle.

KNOWLEDGE MANAGEMENT TOOLS

Knowledge Management tools address an organisation's need for management and processing of information and spreading knowledge. Knowledge Management tools address the requirements of maintaining records and documents electronically. Records are distinguished from documents by the fact that they function as evidence of activities, rather than evidence of intentions. Knowledge Management tools should provide facilities for:

- **Document management:** to support the storage, protection, archiving, classification and retirement of documents and information.
- **Records management:** to support the storage, protection, archiving, classification and retirement of records.
- **Content management:** to support the storage, maintenance and retrieval of documents and information on a system or website. The result is often a knowledge asset represented in written words, figures, graphics and other forms of knowledge presentation.

However, the most important aspect of a Knowledge Management system is the search facility supporting the ability to find information easily, quickly and consistently.

SYLLABUS REFERENCE: ITILMD08-1

Understand and weigh the generic requirements for an integrated set of Service Management technology.

11 IMPLEMENTATION CONSIDERATIONS

LEARNING OBJECTIVES

The purpose of this module is to help candidates to understand implementation considerations, sufficient to enable them to contribute to the implementation of Service Strategy, Service Design, Service Transition, Service Operation or Continual Service Improvement.

SERVICE STRATEGY IMPLEMENTATION ISSUES

Strategic positions are converted into plans with goals and objectives for execution through the Service Lifecycle. The positions are driven by the need to serve specific customers and Market Spaces and influenced by strategic perspectives as a service provider (Figure 11.1).

Plans are a means of achieving these positions. They include the Service Catalogue, Service Pipeline, Contract Portfolio, financial budgets, delivery schedules, and improvement programmes.

Plans ensure that each phase in the Service Lifecycle has the capabilities and resources necessary to reach strategic positions. The Service Lifecycle provides clarity and context for the development of the necessary capabilities and resources.

Plans translate the intent of strategy into action through Service Design, Service Transition, Service Operation and Continual Service Improvement. Service Strategy provides input to each phase of the Service Lifecycle. CSI provides the feedback and learning mechanism by which the execution of strategy is controlled throughout the Lifecycle.

For any given Market Space, Service Strategy defines the portfolio of services to be offered and the customers to be supported. This in turn determines the design, transition and operation capabilities that are required.

New strategic positions are adopted based on patterns that emerge from executing the Service Lifecycle. This bottom-up development of Service Strategy is combined with the traditional top-down approach to form a closed-loop planning and control system for service strategies. Such feedback and learning is a critical success factor for Service Management to drive changes and innovation.

Figure 11.1 Strategic planning and control process [Source: OGC ITIL Service Strategy ISBN 978-0-113310-45-6]

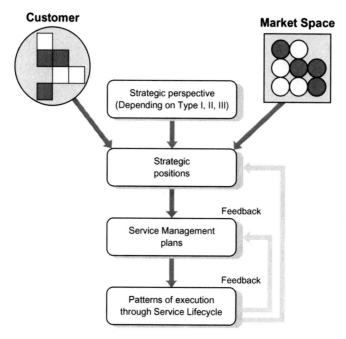

SERVICE DESIGN IMPLEMENTATION ISSUES

The major issues that need to be considered when implementing the Service Design processes are:

- Where do we start?
- How do we improve?
- How do we know we are making progress?

The activities of implementing and improving Service Design need to focus on the needs of the customers and the business. Therefore they should be driven and prioritised by:

- business needs and business impacts;
- risks to the services and processes.

The activities will be influenced by the targets within SLAs and the requirements outlined in the SLRs.

Business Impact Analysis
A valuable source of input when trying to ascertain business needs, impacts and risks is the Business Impact Analysis (BIA). The BIA will dictate the strategy for risk reduction and disaster recovery. Its normal purpose is to identify the effect that a disaster would have on the business. It therefore identifies the most critical business processes and services.

As part of the design phase of a new or changed service, a BIA should be conducted to help define the business continuity strategy and to enable greater understanding of the function and importance of the services. This will enable the organisation to define the critical services, critical business and service periods, cost of loss of services and levels of risk.

Service Level Requirements
As part of the Service Level Management process, the Service Level Requirements (SLRs) for all services will be defined and the ability to deliver against these requirements will be assessed and agreed in a formal SLA. For new services, the requirements must be agreed at the start of the development process, not after completion. Building the service with SLRs uppermost in mind is essential from a Service Design perspective.

Risks to the services and Processes
When implementing the Service Design and other Service Management processes, business-as-usual practices must not be adversely affected. This aspect must be considered during the production and selection of the preferred solution to ensure that disruption to operational services is minimised. This assessment of risk should then be considered in detail in the Service Transition activities as part of the implementation process.

Implementing Service Design
A question often asked is 'Which process shall I implement first?' The real answer is 'All of them' because the true value of implementing all of the Service Management processes is far greater than the sum of the individual Processes. All the Processes are interrelated and, in some cases, are totally dependent on others. What is ultimately required is a single, integrated set of Processes, providing management and control of a set of IT services throughout their entire lifecycle.

While recognising that, to get the complete benefit of implementing Service Management, all of the processes need to be addressed, it is also recognised that it is unlikely that organisations can do everything at once. It is therefore recommended that the areas of greatest need are addressed first. A detailed assessment needs to be undertaken to ascertain the strengths and weaknesses of IT service provision. This should be undertaken by performing customer satisfaction surveys, talking to customers, talking to IT staff and analysing the Processes in action. From this assessment, short-, medium- and long-term strategies can be developed.

It may be that 'quick wins' need to be implemented in the short term to improve the current situation, but these improved Processes may have to be discarded or amended as part of the medium- or long-term strategies. If 'quick wins' are implemented, it is important that they are not done at the expense of the long-term objectives, so these must be considered at all times. However, every organisation will have to start somewhere, and the starting point will be wherever the organisation is now in terms of Service Management maturity.

This means that every organisation should start with an idea of the long-term vision and a review or baseline of the current position. These are the first two steps of the CSI Model, previously described in the CSI approach section.

Measurement of Service Design

There are many measurement methods that can be used to determine the effectiveness and efficiency of the Service Design processes, but all measurements should be consistent with an organisation's CSI policies and methods. The measurement methods and techniques that could be used include:

- **The Balanced Scorecard:** a technique developed by Robert Kaplan and David Norton, and used to measure achievements against objectives from four perspectives – financial, customer, internal processes and learning and growth.

- **Six Sigma:** a technique developed by Motorola, and used to manage variation and eliminate defects.

- **Prerequisites for success (PFSs):** a technique used to ensure that prerequisites required for the successful introduction of new processes are established.

- **Critical Success Factors (CSFs) and Key Performance Indicators (KPIs):** techniques based on:

    - identifying the key elements for establishing a successful Process;
    - establishing appropriate performance measurements for measuring effective Processes.

SYLLABUS REFERENCE: ITILMD09-2

Understand implementation considerations, sufficient to enable candidates to contribute to the implementation of Service Design.

SERVICE TRANSITION IMPLEMENTATION ISSUES

The task for most service provider organisations will be one of service improvement rather than implementation. This is a matter of assessing their current approach to the Service Transition processes and establishing the most effective and efficient improvements to make, prioritised according to the business benefit that can be achieved. All improvements should be completed in line with CSI methods and practices.

The stages of introducing Service Transition will match that of other services, requiring a justification for their introduction (strategic considerations), designing of the Service Transition components and then their introduction to the organisation (transitioning) before they can run in normal mode (operations).

Justifying Service Transition

When setting up Service Transition, attention needs to be paid to ways of quantifying and measuring the benefits, typically as a balance between impact to the business (negative and positive) and cost (in terms of money/staff resources), and in terms of what would be prevented by applying resource to any specific transition, such as diverting staff resources or delaying implementation. Gathering of evidence on the cost of current inadequate Service Transition is a valid and useful exercise, addressing such issues as:

- cost of failed changes;

- extra cost of actual transition compared with budgeted costs;

- errors found in live running that could have been detected during testing.

Designing Service Transition

Factors to be considered when designing Service Transition should include the applicable standards, stakeholder relationships, budgets and resources.

Introducing Service Transition

Experience shows that it is not advisable to attempt to retrofit new transition practices onto projects already under way. The better method is to introduce the new practices into new projects.

Cultural change aspects

It is important that Service Transition staff, those supporting them and those being supported by them, understand and support the new practices. The cultural change programme should also address all other stakeholders.

Risk and value

As with all transitions the associated risks and benefits should be clearly understood and quantified.

SYLLABUS REFERENCE: ITILMD09-3

Understand implementation considerations, sufficient to enable candidates to contribute to the implementation of Service Transition.

SERVICE OPERATION IMPLEMENTATION ISSUES

By the time a service, Process, organisational structure or technology is operating, it has already been implemented. Many of the organisational structures and roles have already been described, so the following is some generic implementation guidance for Service Operation as a whole. Service Operation should strive to deliver stability, but not stagnation! There are many valid reasons why change is a good thing, but Service Operation staff must ensure that changes are absorbed without adverse impact on the stability of quality of services being offered.

Change triggers

There are many triggers for change within Service Operation environments including business imperatives, new, upgraded or obsolescent hardware and software, and legislative, regulatory or governance changes.

Change assessment

Service Operation staff should have early involvement within the Change Management process and should be part of the decision-making process, the scheduling and the implementation.

Measurement of the successful change

The ultimate measure of success is that customers and users experience no variation or outage of service. The effects of the change should be invisible except for any increased functionality or quality resulting from the change.

Other implementation issues that need to be considered include:

- the use of organisational programme and project management methods for the implementation of all infrastructure changes;

- ensuring that all IT staff have early involvement within Service Design and Service Transition activities wherever appropriate;

- ensuring that when Service Management tools are being deployed that the most appropriate tools and licences are used, that the method and timing of the deployment are carefully considered and that the capacity of the infrastructure is checked to ensure that there is sufficient capacity available to support the operation of the new tools.

SYLLABUS REFERENCE: ITILMD09-4

Understand implementation considerations, sufficient to enable candidates to contribute to the implementation of Service Operation.

CONTINUAL SERVICE IMPROVEMENT IMPLEMENTATION ISSUES

CSI can be implemented from two perspectives. First and foremost is the implementation of CSI around services and, secondly, from the perspective of Service Management processes. However, if the Service Management processes are not very mature, then it is often quite difficult to implement the Seven-step Improvement Process because the quality and quantity of data is not available. The main questions to ask when implementing CSI include:

- Are the critical roles identified and in place? These are principally those of CSI Manager, Service Owners, Reporting Analyst and Service Level Manager.

- Where do I start? There are many ways of tackling this, but one of the best is to identify an area of service pain, where a service is consistently not achieving the desired results and address that. Another approach is to consider the Service Lifecycle and look at issues and areas of opportunity with that, particularly around the handover points between the stages. A third approach is to look at particular functions or areas of technology that are causing pain to the organisation and its services.

- Is the IT governance established? It is critical that governance is addressed from a strategic view. Sound IT governance will support the development and transformation to a service-based and process-based organisation and culture supporting the process improvement initiative. CSI needs to become the way of life within the organisation.

- Is organisational change handled effectively? The success of a CSI programme is dependent on the buy-in and support of all stakeholders and appropriate leadership from managers steering and sponsoring the initiative. Using an approach, such as John P Kotter's *Eight Steps to Transforming your Organisation* as follows, will significantly increase the chance of success:

1 Creating a sense of urgency.
2 Forming a guiding coalition.
3 Creating a vision.
4 Communicating the vision.
5 Empowering others to act on the vision.
6 Planning for and creating short-term wins.
7 Consolidating improvements and producing more change.
8 Institutionalising the change.

SYLLABUS REFERENCE: ITILMD09-5

Understand implementation considerations, sufficient to enable candidates to contribute to the implementation of Continual Service Improvement.

SYLLABUS REFERENCE: ITILMD09

Understand implementation considerations, sufficient to enable them to contribute to the implementation of Service Strategy, Service Design, Service Transition, Service Operation or Continual Service Improvement.

12 COMPLEMENTARY INDUSTRY GUIDANCE

LEARNING OBJECTIVES

The purpose of this module is to help candidates to understand how ITIL v3 interfaces with, and can be used alongside, complementary industry guidance including COBIT®, ISO/IEC 20000, Capability Maturity Model® Integration, Balanced Scorecard, Quality Management and the Open Systems Interconnection (OSI) framework.

COBIT®

The COBIT® (Control Objectives for Information and related Technology) framework, produced by the Information Systems Audit and Control Association (ISACA) and managed by the IT Governance Institute, provides a very useful framework of guidance for IT audit and security personnel. The current version of COBIT®, edition 4, includes 34 high-level control objectives which are grouped into four domains:

- plan and organise;
- acquire and implement;
- deliver and support;
- monitor and evaluate.

COBIT® is primarily aimed at auditors, so it has an emphasis on what should be audited and how, rather than including detailed guidance for those who are operating the Processes that will be audited. However, it has a lot of valid material which organisations may find useful. It should be noted that COBIT® and ITIL are not 'competitive', nor are they mutually exclusive. On the contrary, they can be used in conjunction as part of an organisation's overall managerial and governance framework. ITIL provides an organisation with best practice guidance on how to manage and improve its Processes to deliver high-quality, cost-effective IT services. COBIT® provides guidance on how these Processes should be audited and assessed to determine whether they are operating as intended and giving optimum benefit for the organisation.

For a more complete overall picture, candidates may wish to read and become familiar with what COBIT® has to say alongside their reading and understanding of ITIL. Further details of the standard can be found via ISACA at www.isaca.org.

ISO/IEC 20000

In December 2005, the International Organization for Standardization (ISO) launched a formal international standard, ISO/ISE 20000 for IT Service Management, which was based on an earlier British Standard, BS 15000 originally introduced in 2000. This standard contains processes and activities within eight groups:

- management systems;
- planning and implementing service management (PDCA);
- planning and implementing new or changed services;
- service delivery processes;
- relationships processes;
- resolution processes;
- control processes
- release processes.

Organisations can seek independent accreditation for ITSM against the standard. For those organisations seeking formal accreditation to ISO/IEC 20000, there will be significant involvement of staff from all process areas in preparing for and undergoing the formal surveillance necessary to achieve the standard.

Further details of the standard can be found via the itSMF at www.itsmf.com or the ISO at www.iso.org.

CAPABILITY MATURITY MODEL® INTEGRATION

The Capability Maturity Model® Integration (CMMI) is a process improvement approach developed by the Software Engineering Institute (SEI) of Carnegie Mellon University. CMMI gives organisations the essential elements of effective processes. It can be used to guide process improvement across a project, a division or an entire organisation. CMMI helps integrate traditionally separate organisational functions, set process improvement goals and priorities, provide guidance for quality processes and provide a point of reference for appraising current processes. For more information, see http://www.sei.cmu.edu/cmmi/.

A number of IT consultancies have built the maturity model into their ITSM assessment services as a way of assisting organisations prepare for and judge process improvements, including those in the Service Operation area. Organisations may wish to use some form of the model to help drive their path towards independent ISO/IEC 20000 certification.

BALANCED SCORECARD

A new approach to strategic management was developed in the early 1990s by Dr Robert Kaplan (Harvard Business School) and Dr David Norton. They named this system the 'Balanced Scorecard'. Recognising some of the weaknesses and vagueness of previous management approaches, the Balanced Scorecard approach provides a clear prescription as to what companies should measure in order to 'balance' the financial perspective. The Balanced Scorecard suggests that the organisation is viewed from four perspectives, and it is valuable to develop metrics, collect data and analyse achievements relative to each of these perspectives:

- The Learning and Growth Perspective;
- The Business Process Perspective;
- The Customer Perspective;
- The Financial Perspective.

Many organisations choose to use the Balanced Scorecard method as a way of assessing and reporting their IT quality performance. Further details are available through the Balanced Scorecard User Community at www.scorecardsupport.com.

QUALITY MANAGEMENT

There are distinct advantages of linking an organisation's ITSM processes to its quality management system. If an organisation has a formal quality management system such as ISO 9000, Six Sigma, Total Quality Management (TQM) etc., then this can be used to assess progress regularly and drive forward agreed service improvement initiatives through regular reviews and reporting. Many organisations have used a regular annual audit or external assessment as a way of determining the required improvements and then their quality management system to drive through the specific programmes of work.

ITIL AND THE OSI FRAMEWORK

At around the time that ITIL v1 was being written, the International Organization for Standardization (ISO) launched an initiative that resulted in the Open Systems Interconnection (OSI) framework. Since this initiative covered many of the same areas as ITIL, it is not surprising that they covered much of the same ground. However, it is also not surprising that they classified their processes differently, used different terminology, or used the same terminology in different ways.

To confuse matters even more, it is common for different groups in an organisation to use terminology from both ITIL and the OSI framework.

Although it is not in the scope of this book to explore the OSI framework, it has made significant contributions to the definition and execution of ITSM programmes and projects around the world. It has also caused a great deal of debate between teams that do not realise the origins of the terminology that they are using. For example, some organisations have two Change Management departments: one following the ITIL Change Management process and the other using the OSI's Installations, Moves, Additions and Changes (IMAC) model. Each department is convinced that it is completely different from the other, and that they perform different roles. Closer examination will reveal that there are several areas of commonality.

SYLLABUS REFERENCE: ITILMD10

Understand how ITIL v3 interfaces and can be used alongside complementary industry practice.

INDEX

205

User Profiles (UPs), 63
Utility,
  automation and, 185
  costs, 21
  creation of value, 36
  definition, 13–14
utility-based provisioning model, 70

validation *see* Service Validation
  and Testing

value, 5, 13, 36
  creation, 35, 41, Fig. 4.1, Fig. 5.1
  customer assets and, 36, 45–46,
    Fig. 5.2, Fig. 5.3, Fig. 5.20
  see also service valuation
Value on Investment (VOI),
  22, 175
Value Networks, 41–42, 51,
  Fig. 5.7, Fig. 5.8
VOI *see* Value on Investment

warning events, 149
Warranty,
  automation and, 185
  costs, 52
  creation of value, 36
  definition, 14

zero-based funding, 71